World-Famous

PROPHECIES

& Predictions

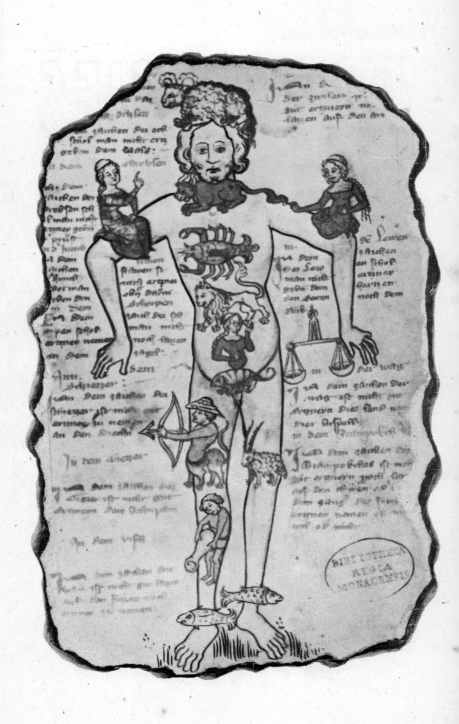

World-Famous

PROPHECIES
& Predictions

Ashok Kumar Sharma

PUSTAK MAHAL®
DELHI·BANGALORE·MUMBAI·PATNA·HYDERABAD

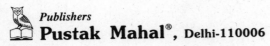

Publishers
Pustak Mahal®, Delhi-110006

Sales Centres
- 6686, Khari Baoli, Delhi-110006, *Ph:* 23944314, 23911979
- 10-B, Netaji Subhash Marg, Daryaganj, New Delhi-110002
  Ph: 23268292, 23268293, 23279900 • *Fax:* 011-23280567
  E-mail: rapidexdelhi@indiatimes.com

Administrative Office
J-3/16 (Opp. Happy School), Daryaganj, New Delhi-110002
Ph: 23276539, 23272783, 23272784 • *Fax:* 011-23260518
E-mail: info@pustakmahal.com • *Website:* www.pustakmahal.com

Branch Offices
BANGALORE: 22/2, Mission Road (Shama Rao's Compound),
Bangalore-560027, *Ph:* 22234025 • *Fax:* 080-22240209
E-mail: pmblr@sancharnet.in • pustak@sancharnet.in

MUMBAI: 23-25, Zaoba Wadi (Opp. VIP Showroom), Thakurdwar,
Mumbai-400002, *Ph:* 22010941 • *Fax:* 022-22053387
E-mail: rapidex@bom5.vsnl.net.in

PATNA: Khemka House, 1st Floor (Opp. Women's Hospital), Ashok
Rajpath, Patna-800004 , *Ph:* 3094193 • *Telefax:* 0612-2302719
E-mail: rapidexptn@rediffmail.com

HYDERABAD: 5-1-707/1, Brij Bhawan, Bank Street, Koti,
Hyderabad-500095, *Telefax:* 040-24737290
E-mail: pustakmahalhyd@yahoo.co.in

© **Pustak Mahal, 6686, Khari Baoli, Delhi-110006**

ISBN 81-223-0551-2

Edition : 2005

Printed at : Param Offsetters, Okhla, New Delhi-110020

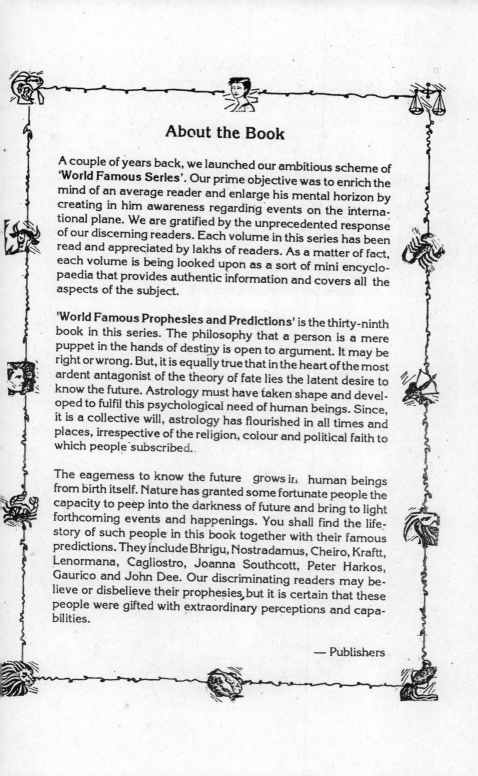

About the Book

A couple of years back, we launched our ambitious scheme of 'World Famous Series'. Our prime objective was to enrich the mind of an average reader and enlarge his mental horizon by creating in him awareness regarding events on the international plane. We are gratified by the unprecedented response of our discerning readers. Each volume in this series has been read and appreciated by lakhs of readers. As a matter of fact, each volume is being looked upon as a sort of mini encyclopaedia that provides authentic information and covers all the aspects of the subject.

'World Famous Prophesies and Predictions' is the thirty-ninth book in this series. The philosophy that a person is a mere puppet in the hands of destiny is open to argument. It may be right or wrong. But, it is equally true that in the heart of the most ardent antagonist of the theory of fate lies the latent desire to know the future. Astrology must have taken shape and developed to fulfil this psychological need of human beings. Since, it is a collective will, astrology has flourished in all times and places, irrespective of the religion, colour and political faith to which people subscribed.

The eagerness to know the future grows in human beings from birth itself. Nature has granted some fortunate people the capacity to peep into the darkness of future and bring to light forthcoming events and happenings. You shall find the life-story of such people in this book together with their famous predictions. They include Bhrigu, Nostradamus, Cheiro, Kraftt, Lenormana, Cagliostro, Joanna Southcott, Peter Harkos, Gaurico and John Dee. Our discriminating readers may believe or disbelieve their prophesies, but it is certain that these people were gifted with extraordinary perceptions and capabilities.

— Publishers

CONTENTS

The Hidden Capacity to Foretell

The fortune-tellers use different methods to predict the future. Some read the lines on the palms, forehead and even the sole. Others rely on ancient texts, gaze in a crystal or use tarot cards. There are people who predict the future by studying a person's handwriting. To most of us this seems bewildering and mysterious. A question arises in the mind — can anybody peep into the future and — if so, to what extent? There have been exhaustive researches on this subject throughout the world. These researches have brought out one startling conclusion that every man possesses a latent capacity to tell the future. It may vary from person to person, but it is doubtless there. This is even acknowledged by science.

The doctors and psychologists in Great Britain launched a novel research in 1947. The subject was — Does an ordinary man possess the capacity to unravel the future? Attempts were also made to study the mysterious and puzzling aspects of human personality. This study was carried out by well-known physicians and psychotherapists. They decided that they would keep detailed records of their dreams for the next few weeks. The dreams recorded by them were to be sent to the Jung Institute in Zurich. Details regarding dreams were collected in seventeen other countries of the world in the same manner.

A strange fact emerged from the study. It was found that it was possible to foresee future by collating information provided by the dreams.

9

It should be kept in mind that the members of this study group were not even known to each other intimately. One member dreamt of an accident. The second person saw an aeroplane falling down at a rapid pace near the Shannon aerodrome. Another person dreamt that a plane was disintegrating and it belonged to KLM, the Dutch airlines. A similar dream was seen by the leader of this study group, Dr. Alice Buck. She tried to remember the time of the accident in her dream. It flashed in her mind, it was three in the morning. The data provided by these dreams were minutely analysed and the authorities were fore-warned. But, the inevitable had to happen and it did happen.

A majority of this group had seen this dream, after midnight around 3.40 a.m. on the night between 2nd and 3rd September, 1954. The surprising thing is that this dream turned into a reality within twenty four hours. The next day, exactly at that hour, a KLM plane crashed near the Shannon airport.

An enquiry was instituted into the dreams of the members of this study group. One person had dreamt that some lengthy thing was lying in slush and many people were shouting for help, hanging to it for their dear life. Another researcher saw that a plane was being filled with slush and a third person dreamt that the dead bodies were being taken out of the slush.

Shannon river flows by the side of the accident site. Muddy water entered the plane following the accident. An officer had to cross the marshy site to inform the police and then only the rescue team reached the site. The rescue team found many passengers hanging from the tail of the plane. Their voice had become hoarse due to continuous shouting.

This very study group had informed the authorities well in advance regarding the plane disasters at Singapore and Naples. These accidents took place on March 12, 1954 and April 8, 1954 respectively. Unfortunately, these studies were not taken seriously at that time and hence no efforts or precautions were taken to prevent these accidents.

Another such project was undertaken by the end of the year 1966. Dr. J.C. Barker concluded that generally every person has a hidden capacity to know the future, however limited it may be. Usually, this capacity is very weak and hence any premonition regarding a coming event is known to him only a little time before it actually happens, and as such he can do little to prevent it. Dr. Barker believed that a man comes to know of his imminent death sometime before death actually strikes.

10

Dr. Barker had also toured the mining areas of South Wales in England. He also went to Aberfan, where a huge mound of coal slags had flattened the building of Pentglas Junior and Infants School. These slag heaps are common sight in the mining areas. These mounds are called 'coal tips'. It is a common practice to dump low grade coal, stones and muck at the mouth of mines. Years of dumping results in their assuming the shape of huge mounds that look like hills from a distance. In Aberfan, the mounds of pit waste had assumed massive proportions after seventy years of dumping. This huge mound of coal slag was nearly 8000 feet in height. Directly below it was the village of Aberfan whose total population was about 5,000. Constant fear lurked into the minds of the villagers that one day, this huge dump of coal slag will crash down on their houses and wipe out the entire village.

Their worst fears turned out to be true one day. This huge mound of two million tons of slag slid down half a mile and engulfed the school and nearby houses. 116 children and 28 adults were crushed to death. Nearly, all children between the age of nine and eleven of this village died in this accident.

Dr. Barker collected all information regarding this terrible incident through *Evening Standard*, a local newspaper. He got response from

A two million ton mound of coal slag crashed down and flattened the building of Pentglass School.

11

76 persons. Amongst them 60 people had alluded to a feeling amongst the children of the school that coal was raining on them. They had this feeling two days prior to the actual accident. They felt that they were being crushed under coal slags. The elders thought that the children were telling them a concocted story to avoid going to school. Many mothers had also seen such a dream but they did not pay any attention to it as they did not believe that such a thing could happen.

During the investigation, it was found that at least twenty two persons had also dreamt about this incident. They had told others about it and did not send their wards to school on that fateful day. Amongst them was one Mrs. Grace Engleton who lived at Sidcup in Kent. On October 14, 1966, she saw in her dream that a huge mountain of coal was falling on the children. Terrified children were screaming ... running to and fro ... and were being killed.

... And on October 21, 1966, this heart-rending disaster took place in the mining area of Aberfan in a similar manner absolutely.

It is not possible for everyone to read the future. Peter Fairley, Science Editor of *Evening Standard* ran a special column in his paper for one year from January, 1967. Prophesies received from readers were published in this column. 469 prophesies regarding accidents, disasters, political events and crimes were published in this column. Only a few persons were found to have the natural gift of being soothsayers. Amongst these people a few persons had prophesied correctly regarding 18 matters. *Evening Standard* published details regarding these persons on March 11, 1968.

Amongst the eighteen correct prophesies, seven had been made by two persons. One was Lorna Middleton, a piano teacher and resident of Edmonton. She was aged 53. The other person was 44 years old Allen Hencher who was an operator in a post office. On enquiry, it was found that these two persons had never made any prophesies previous to those sent to *Evening Standard*. They also had no intention to follow the occupation of fortune-tellers. Hencher's prophesies were very remarkable. He had not seen the three aeroplane accidents, one train accident and and a bank dacoity, about which he had prophesied in dreams. He had seen them while fully awake and in a state of trance.

After an extensive research for a year, it was found that some people have a premonition regarding coming events. They do not make

12

Nasser

Ted Kennedy

any efforts in the direction but this knowledge comes to them automatically. On the other hand, there are people who get this knowledge regarding future occurrences in their dreams.

After lapse of some time, Robert Nelson initiated similar studies in America. His study was started in June, 1968. Nelson received some 600 prophesies in the course of one year. On June 23, 1969, a lady from Pennsylvania sent details of an unfortunate incident involving another member of the Kennedy family. She chose to remain anonymous. She wrote, "There would be an explosion in water and a fire would break out. Perhaps, the time of Ted Kennedy is up." Exactly a month after, Ted Kennedy died in an accident. Everything happened in the same manner as that woman had prophesied. There was an explosion, a river and fire exactly as it had been foretold by that unknown woman.

A woman was reading a newspaper in Bridgeport on August 17, 1970. She was glancing through a news regarding President Nasser of Egypt. Suddenly, she felt that Nasser was soon going to die of a heart attack. For three days, she did not mention about this uneasy feeling to anyone. Eventually, she became so tense that she wrote to Nelson about her premonition. Nelson got this letter on September 21, and on September 28, the whole world was shocked to hear the news of Nasser's death after a heart attack.

The headmaster of a Primary school in New York, astounded the world by publishing his study in December, 1978. Twenty five years ago, when he was an ordinary teacher, he had asked his students to write an essay on what the children thought of the world twenty five years hence. The students of class V tried to envisage the world after 25 years in 1953. Richard Arback, the teacher kept the essays of the students in safe custody for twenty five years. When they were analysed in 1978, it was found that those children of fifth standard had successfully imagined what the world would be after a lapse of 25 years.

From researches carried out in Cambridge University between 1936 and 1976, it has been ascertained that an ordinary man can predict future events quite correctly to a limited extent. American scientists have also done research on this subject. They have also come to the conclusion that ordinary people have the capacity to forsee the future. If one forms that habit of analysing things, taking into account the circumstances prevailing at that time, he can sharpen his capacity to predict future events in a convincing and competent manner.

There is a simple way to peep into the future. One should intensely concentrate on any question and ponder, if it is like this at present, what will it be like in future. One can easily develop one's inner power by meditating over matters.

The gist of all researches carried out on this subject all over the world is that mass efforts in this direction are more efficacious than individual attempts. In certain matters, several people were asked to prophesy about a problem. Then the same question was tackled on a collective scale. The results of both the processes were then analysed and a conclusion was arrived at.

Now, the question arises as to what is the method employed by the fortune. Firstly, the fortune-teller studies all aspects of the problem about which he has to make a prediction. This is done patiently in an ordinary and common manner. Then they concentrate on it to get some premonition. This is done in a calm atmosphere. Initially, one has to analyse as to how one arrived at correct answers in the past. The same method can then be followed.

David Loe, the Director of Institute of Future Forecasting of California University in Los Angeles is convinced that everyone has some capacity to fore-tell things. Only one requires a little practice to successfully peep into the future and predict. ■ ■

14

The Oracles of Delphi

Greece was the centre of ancient human civilisation. The very mention of its name brings to mind warriors like Alexander and philosophers like Socrates and Aristotle. There was a mysterious temple in Greece, which was famous for correct predictions regarding future. Great rulers like Alexander, Nero and Croesus as also illustrious poets like Homer went there to know their future. Today the temple is in ruins but at one time its splendour was colossal. Holy priestesses sat in the temple to make predictions and solve the problems of those who sought their help.

Alexander stood face to face with the priestess. 'Alexander is not used to hear refusals.' Priestess, tell me what the future holds for me?' Thundered the great warrior. He was fully clad in armour and had a steel helmet on his head.

"Pythia is not anybody's slave. You are standing in the temple of Apollo. You are just an ordinary human being. Go away," replied the old and ugly priestess (Pythia), "This is not the time to make predictions."

Alexander flew into a rage and held Pythia by her arm, nearly dragging her and said, "There can be no limitation of time for Alexander. Do not make me more angry otherwise it shall cause havoc. Go into the temple to meditate and tell me how I shall fare in the future."

Pythia was nearly breathless. She controlled herself and wrung herself free. "If you insist on knowing then listen," she said, "You will

15

Alexander, the Great, whose early death was predicted by the Pythia of Delphi temple.

be acclaimed as the conqueror of the world. But, you shall die in a foreign country in a pitiable condition. You are not to live long, but even your enemies will utter your name with profound respect."

Alexander remained silent for a second and then shouted, "Listen, O holy Jupiter, God of Fortune. I am satisfied that I am fated to be a world conqueror and people will remember me with respect. The rest is just immaterial to me. I do not want to know it, and as I do not want that it shall ever happen."

Alexander then returned to his kingdom. History bears testimony to the fact that he fought a number of wars and won them. He conquered many lands, but could not live long. This World-Conqueror, who once expressed his sorrow that there were no more countries for him to subdue,

Funeral procession of Alexander. Pythia had forecast correctly.

died at an early age of thirty three. He died in a foreign land due to high fever caused by infected injuries. Pythia had correctly foretold his future.

This incident tells us that there were fortune tellers in ancient Greece even 356 years before the birth of Christ. There used to be a temple of Apollo in the hilly regions of Delphi. This place was on sea-shore and a little distance away from Athens. The ruins of this temple are still extant. The business of predicting future used to be conducted in this temple for twenty four hours on specified days. When one fortune teller got tired, another came to continue the work.

Diodorus Siculus, a Greek historian, has written, "Delphi was discovered by wandering goats. When the shepherds took them for grazing, the goats behaved in a very peculiar manner after eating the grass growing in a fissure in the earth. A shepherd entered the crevice to find out the reason of this abnormal behaviour of the goats. This shepherd started telling the future of the other shepherds as he entered the crevice. Somehow, the capacity to foretell future was attained as soon as one entered this crevice. It was very mysterious and intriguing.

Gradually, the story of the remarkable power of the crevice spread in the region. The people of the area started flocking to this crevice to take

The ruins of the holy temple of Apollo in Delphi, Greece.

17

advice regarding their problems and difficulties. They also took advice regarding future events. Some curious people who went inside the crevice never returned. To prevent such accidents, a woman was deputed there. She also undertook the task of predicting the future of people who wished to know about it. A temple was erected on the site and a wooden platform was provided to that woman so that she was protected from the vagaries of the weather and had a place to sit on and do her work. Steam came out of the crevice as the woman (priestess) made predictions. She was completely enveloped by the steam coming out of the crevice. The platform on which the priestess sat was supported by three pillars.

When the worship of God Apollo started in this temple, the priestess was given the nomenclature of Pythia. According to Diodorous, only virgins were appointed as Pythias in this temple. The first Pythia was a girl named Phemonoe. Historians believe that Phemonoe was appointed Pythia in 700 B.C. Many young girls were appointed as Pythia after the first one. It was only after a tragic incident that decision was taken to appoint only women over fifty years of age as Pythia.

When Alexander went to Delphi, an old Pythia was working there. It proves that this decision to appoint only old women as Pythia must have been taken during the last two hundred years. The reason was that a young man named Echecrates had come to enquire about his future. He raped the pretty and young Pythia. Pythia had told him that he would be killed after committing a crime. He was killed immediately after committing the crime of raping Pythia. From that time only old women were employed for the task of telling the future.

Another historian, Plutarch, has testified, "When I went there, the current Pythia belonged to the most respected and high status family. She was performing the task of predicting the future with such ease and accuracy that one could hardly believe it. Before and during the period when these priestesses worked, they were tested by sprinkling cold water on them. Those priestesses who shivered when the water fell on them, were removed."

During the time of Plutarch (100 B.C.) there was only one Pythia at Delphi. But in 500 B.C. when this temple was at the peak of its popularity, there were three Pythias working there. When one got tired, another one took her place. The famous historian, Flavius Philotratus, has written that a temple of stones was built from the donations given by

18

Nero had ordered live entombment of all the priests of Delphi when insulted by the Pythia.

devotees. This temple was destroyed by fire in 548 B.C. It was soon rebuilt between 530 and 514 B.C. Emperor Amasis of Egypt gave a lot of monetary help.

The Roman emperor Nero thought of paying a visit to Delphi during A.D. 63-65. Due to pressure of work he could visit it only in A.D. 67. He reached there after a long and tiring journey. As soon as Nero entered the temple, the Pythia present there screamed, "Get out, go away, killer of your mother. Beware of the figure of 73." Nero felt outraged. He immediately ordered that the priests and that Pythia be buried alive after their hands and legs had been chopped off. When these unfortunate people were being buried, Nero was himself supervising the destruction of the temple.

Nero thought that Pythia had predicted that he would live till the age of 73. But, Pythia meant something different Nero was killed next year and he was succeeded by Galba who was aged seventy three years.

The Roman Philosopher Cicero who did not believe in God, predictions and destiny has written, "The prosperity, splendour and respect that Delphi enjoys is due to the remarkable genius of the fortune-tellers of the temple. From times immemorial, royalty as well as common man has come there from different countries ... and the reason of their collecting there is apparent."

19

The Roman philosopher, Cicero, who did not believe in destiny, had to acknowledge the genius of the priestesses of Delphi-in forecasting future.

In the beginning, people gathered on the seventh of the month to know about their future. Later on, it was decided to fix the seventh day of every week for this purpose. Hence, 7th, 14th, 21st and 28th day of the month were selected when the predictions were to be made.

The work load of Pythia fortune-tellers kept on increasing. It was then decided to organise a fortune-telling fair every year during the birth-day celebrations of Apollo in spring. The work of prediction also continued on the seventh day of the month on a smaller scale. Gradually, the fees for making predictions also increased. After some time, people started complaining that it was becoming beyond their pecuniary capacity. As a result, collective and mass fortune-telling sessions were organised. In these assemblies, Pythia used to sit on the steps of the temple and the crowd would sit on the floor before her. A question and answer session then ensued.

Philosopher Plutarch is also known as a priest of Apollo. He has written, "An ill-omen occurred when some foreigners came there. The sacrificial goat did not shiver when holy water was sprinkled on her. She stood still. It was supposed that God Apollo would accept her only when she shivered in a particular manner. The priests did not pay attention to this phenomenon and sacrificed it. As a result, when Pythia was brought there, she could not give even one correct answer. After some time she shrieked loudly and became unconscious. After some time she died."

Such incidents were rare. But, whenever such an incident happened, the people of Delphi honestly recorded it in contemporary history. The work of predicting future was carried out in the following manner as inscribed in these records.

People desirous of knowing the future paid the prescribed fees. Then they, deposited their questions in chresmographeon, which was the office of the temple. This office prepared a list in which the details regarding the person and his questions were given. The associate priest, known as Hosioi, then went to the chief priest with the list. The chief priest then asked Pythia about the question and the person was called in and given answers to his queries.

For the ritual of forecasting, Pythia had to observe a fast for the day, bathe and come in white clothes. If the sacrificial goat shivered and bleated when the holy water was sprinkled on it, it was taken and sacrificed at the altar. Pythia was then adorned with a crown made of a special creeper and leaves of Apollo plant. Barley and leaves of laurel plant were burnt in a special vessel before Pythia. Pythia also chewed the leaves of laurel. She then started swinging in a trance.

The questioner was also purified by sprinkling holy water on him. After he had paid the prescribed fee and donation, he was given a cake

Pythia forecasting future. She sat on a three-legged stool.

Homer, the great poet, was told in Delphi that he would achieve eternal fame.

like thing by the temple workers. He had to keep it in a special place outside the temple. People coming from outside had to hire a helper who helped them in performing all the necessary rituals. The questioner was made to sacrifice a goat near an oven after sprinkling holy water on it. Pythia answered his queries from behind a curtain in the temple.

The great Greek poet Homer was blind. He also went to Delphi. When he asked about his future, he got this answer, "The humanity will never forget you." This proved to be absolutely correct. The period between 1100 B.C. and 900 B.C. is regarded as the period of Homer. His book *Iliad* and *Odyssey* have immortalised him for ever.

From 700 B.C. to 300 B.C. Pythia continued to predict the future at Delphi. During this period, many Pythias proved their genius in doing this work. Some six hundred years before Christ, Croesus of Lydia and Emperor Cyrus of Persia did not see eye to eye. Croesus even thought of attacking Persia. He wanted to confirm from the Pythia at Delphi if he would be victorious over Cyrus. He sent a messenger to Delphi. He instructed him to first ask her a question to test her accuracy. He told him to ask Pythia as to what Croesus did ten days after the messenger left for Delphi. Pythia replied, "The emperor cooked the meat of a sheep and tortoise in a brass vessel and then poured sand over it and covered with a brass lid."

The messenger returned from Delphi and conveyed Pythia's reply. Croesus was overjoyed to hear this as Pythia had correctly told what he had done. He sent his ambassador to Delphi with huge amounts of gold, jewels and costly presents and clothes as gift for the temple. This time Pythia gave the following answer to his question regarding war with Cyrus.

If you cross river Helois

Then listen Emperor Croesus,

A big empire will be destroyed.

The ambassador also asked her regarding the duration of the reign of Croesus and who would be his successor? If the dumb prince would ever be able to speak up? Whom should he befriend for attacking Persia. The answer was:

The reign shall last,

Till a mule ascends the throne,

If the dumb prince regains his voice,

A calamity shall follow, the kingdom will be gone.

Alliance should be forged before the fight,

With a Greek ruler who has the most might.

Croesus will come out alive from the fire,

But, without doubt, shall lose the empire.

The ambassador returned and told the Emperor about Pythia's predictions. Croesus thought that the predictions were in his favour. He formed alliance with the most powerful Greek kingdom of Sparta and attacked Persia. Croesus faced untold difficulties as he crossed the river

The tomb of Cyrus.

Cyrus: Being son of a Persian father and Egyptian mother, he was referred to as cross-breed mule.

Helois. The Persian soldiers decimated his army. The empire of Lydia disintegrated. When armed soldiers entered the palace of Croesus, the dumb prince screamed in terror, " Has Croesus been killed."

The victorious Emperor Cyrus had a Persian father and Egyptian mother. He was always referred to as a mixed breed mule behind his back. After capturing the city of Lydia, he ordered that Croesus and his fourteen loyal officers be burnt at stake. The fire was lighted. Croesus called out to the famous philosopher Solon, "You were right Solon." When Cyrus enquired why he was saying this, Croesus replied, "Solon told me that there is no greater pleasure than death."

Cyrus was so pleased with this statement that he forgave Croesus. But, the soldiers could not put out the fire. Suddenly, it started raining and the fire got extinguished. Croesus had come out alive from the fire as per the prediction.

The last predictions in Delphi were made in the year A.D 362. The temple was in ruins and the holy spring flowing inside the temple had dried up. This spring was sealed on the orders of Roman Emperor Hadrian after he had heard some predictions from the then Pythia. Pythia had predicted that Hadrian will become Emperor of Rome. Hadrian was

24

The Roman Emperor Hadrian: He not only got the holy spring closed, but destroyed the entire temple of Delphi.

worried that some one might dethrone him after getting the same blessings in Delphi. He had the temple destroyed.

Emperor Julian sent his physician to Delphi in A.D 362. The then Pythia who was sick took her round the ruined temple and said, "People will always remember Delphi and Pythia, but the great Roman Empire will be reduced to dust." This prediction of the sick Pythia also proved to be absolutely true. ■ ■

The Mysterious fortune-Tellers of Egypt

Many ancient texts reveal that in the hoary past, the Egyptians used modern methods for forecasting the future. There were many temples in that country, where people gathered to know about their future. Mention can be made of the temples at Karnak and Luxor on the banks of river Nile. Their ruins stand even today as mute witnesses of their past splendour. Along with forecasting, these temples were also centres for treatment of the sick people. In many cases inner power was used to treat people. It is amazing how such correct predictions were made at that time. It shall for ever remain a mystery that can never be unravelled.

Pharaoh Thutmos-III of Egypt sat kneeling at the altar of the Akhetaton temple near Memphis. He had come to know the future from the holy saint of that temple. The Pharaoh desired to expand his empire and wanted to know if he would succeed. His query was, "O! holy saint, will my expedition be successful?"

The reply was, "Definitely yes. You shall extend your empire up to river Euphrates. You shall capture two countries in the south as also a country full of gold mines. Many slaves would be captured, but the emperor will suffer eight injuries that would take a long time to heal. The hereditary friends of Pharaoh shall achieve immortality during this war."

After ascertaining the predictions from the saint of the temple of Akhetaton near Memphis, the Emperor launched an attack towards the south of the river Nile. He was successful in conquering vast lands which in the present times form part of Palestine and Syria. Not only that, he was able to subdue Nubia which was renowned as the land of gold mines. The

Historical documents reveal the existence of the famous temples at Karnak and Luxor in the time of Pharaoh Joser. Their ruins can still be seen.

Pharaoh Thutmos-III, crossed the river Nile to attack territories in South, only after getting assurances of victory from the saint of Akhetaton temple.

saint of Akhetaton had predicted correctly. A lot of slaves were captured and everything predicted by the saint came to pass as prophesied.

The temples of Akhetaton, Philae, Thebes and Adfu were renowned in ancient Egypt. These temples were situated on the banks of river Nile. From 600 B.C. to 200 B.C., these temples were not only centres of worship, but the priests of these temples also made prophesies regarding future events. Curious people thronged them to know about their future and destiny.

The authentic and authoritative researches have proved that there were temples of Karnak and Luxor on the banks of Nile near the city of Thebes. Apart from making prophesies, these temples also catered to the needs of the sick people, where they were treated for their ailments. It is

27

The famous temple of Luxor situated on the banks of river Nile. Apart from forecasting, sick people were given treatment in this temple.

recorded that some officers were sent to administer these temples in or around 2800 B.C. by Pharaoh Joser. A fight ensued between them for some unknown reasons.

An inscription in an ancient Egyptian document of about 1750 B.C. still remains controversial. There have been many discussions regarding its import. From its language, it seems to be a record of events, while from its style it can also be treated as a document making a prophesy. We reproduce it below:

"People have revolted against Pharaohs appointed by God himself. The capital city has been ravaged. The poor slaves have imprisoned the Emperor. High ranking officers are fleeing to save their lives. Many government officials have been killed. The documents regarding tax and revenue have been destroyed. The poor are in possession of palaces. The rich have been rendered penniless. Those who did not even possess a goat are now in possession of hordes of oxen. Beggars are distributing grains. Slaves have become masters." Historians and archaeologists have acute differences regarding this inscription. Some people believe that it depicts the conditions prevailing at that time, when the slaves had captured the capital city in a revolt during the reign of the father of Pharaoh

28

Thutmos I. Some historians discount this theory as baseless for the following reasons.

They assert that the above document is not a record of events, otherwise there would have been some mention of crushing of the revolt of the slaves after which the Pharaohs regained their kingdom. It seems that some Pharaoh must have asked some soothsayer about the future. The predictions of the fortune-teller must have been recorded. It is certain that such a prophesy could not have been made orally. Whatever may be the case, it is true that an unsuccessful revolt by the slaves took place in the year 1750 B.C. and is part of history.

The fortune-tellers believed that a time would come when the dead would be revived. That is why, the bodies of influential persons in Egypt were mummified and kept in the pyramids. It will not be surprising if this prophesy regarding revival of dead persons proves true some day in view of the rapid and far-reaching progress taking place in the field of medicines. Nowadays, many rich and prosperous persons are having their bodies preserved after getting them embalmed by scientific methods.

It would be pertinent to recall a prophesy made regarding Emperor Cyrus. His kingdom was near the sea. Once Cyrus went to the temple at Thebes to know about his future. This priest told him that during an expedition his head will be soaked in blood but he would have no injury in

The revolt of the slaves.

29

Darius who conquered Egypt as forecasted.

The ruins of Karnak temple which was famous for predicting future.

the head. His nose and ears will be full of blood, but it shall not be his blood. His skull would be in a river of blood, but his body would be safe. The Persians will be stronger under him and Babylon and Egypt will not remain under the Pharaohs but will be ruled by the Persians.

This prophesy made near about sixth century B.C. seems to be very confusing. It was made by an unknown fortune-teller. About 530 B.C. Cyrus was killed in an expedition he led in Middle East. His head was cut off and kept in a big leather bag, commonly called *mashak*. This *mashak* was full of blood of some animal. It was then only that people could realise the relevance of that confusing prophesy made regarding Cyrus. Before the event, it must have seemed to be a conundrum to the people.

Later, the Persian soldiers conquered Egypt under the leadership of Darius I. Darius is considered as one of the greatest of Persian rulers. His kingdom extended from Egypt to the Indus river in India. The prophesy was thus fulfilled. ■ ■

30

Bhrigu: Surveyor of Past, Present & Future

There have been many fortune-tellers who could correctly predict the future of people living at that time. Can you envisage a fortune-teller who could prophesy the future of people to be born in the coming centuries. Not only that, his book contains the past, present and future of every individual. Such a prophetic fortune-teller was the Indian savant Maharishi Bhrigu. It is said that any person can know about his past life and future by consulting the book Bhrigu-Samhita written by him. It seems that he had some divine power to see the future of all in the same manner as you can see through a wall of glass. Many people have testified regarding the amazing accuracy of the predictions read out to them from this book. Not only that, events of their past life are also unfolded.

B *hrigu-Samhita* is supposed to be the original book of astrology. This book contains details regarding the past, present and future life of all. Those who have faith in astrology have great respect for this book and nearly revere it. They have complete faith in what the book tells them about their future. In short, this book can be described as the *Bible* of Indian fortune-tellers.

On the other hand, there are many people who do not believe in the existence of *Bhrigu-Samhita* and even deny that any person named Bhrigu ever lived. According to them the so-called *Bhrigu-Samhita* is nothing but an attempt by astrologers to defraud the gullible and superstitious people under a well laid conspiracy. They assert that the entire book is nothing but a fake account. The astrologers earned their living through this book and even today their descendants are making hay because of this book. They are simply taking advantage of the desire of ordinary people to know their future. It is nothing but psychological exploitation of the simple and gullible people in a systematic manner.

Regarding the writing of *Bhrigu-Samhita*, there is a mythological story. It runs like this. Once, the gods differed as to who was the greatest amongst Brahma, Vishnu and Mahesh, the Hindu trinity. They could not come to any conclusion and approached *Maharishi* Bhrigu to settle their dispute.

Bhrigu thought over the matter and said, "It is impossible to make a guess or hasty judgement in the matter. I will personally test them and decide." Bhrigu thought that the one who could control his temper should be the best of the lot. He was able to enrage both Brahma and Mahesh. Lastly he went to test Vishnu. Vishnu was asleep on his bed of *Sheshnag* in *Kshirsagar*. Lakshmi, the goddess of wealth, was massaging his legs. Bhrigu stood for some time and then a plan flashed into his mind. He hit the sleeping Vishnu on the chest with his feet. Vishnu was naturally awakened. He did not lose his composure and said, "*Brahmrishi*, my chest is hard like armour. I hope your feet are not hurt."

Bhrigu had no other option but to declare Vishnu as the greatest amongst the trinity. Vishnu did not mind that Bhrigu had hit him like that, but, Lakshmi could not stomach the insult to her husband. Getting angry,

The Bhrigu-Samhita was written with the blessings of Lord Vishnu.

32

she cursed Bhrigu in these words. "O haughty brahmin, listen, in future no brahmin will be wealthy and this includes you."

Bhrigu had completed his *magnum opus* '*Jyotish-Samhita*' by that time. Fate and destiny of all had been determined in that book for the coming centuries. He replied, "Wealth shall rain on the house that has my blessings."

Lakshmi was further enraged. She said, "Then, remember, you are so proud of your book in which you have already prophesied the future of all. Now, I curse that your predictions will never be correct."

It was now the turn of Bhrigu to get angry. He thought of cursing Lakshmi when Vishnu intervened. He said, "Do not be sad and angry, O *maharishi*. I shall grant you divine insight. You write another treatise. It will never go wrong." It is presumed that *Bhrigu-Samhita* was written as a result of this gift granted by Lord Vishnu.

In this modern age, every mythological story is being tested at the touchstone of reality. Even, if we accept that the above story is imaginary and allegorical, it at least points out to the fact that a savant named Bhrigu lived in the hoary past. Not only that, it confirms that due to his knowledge and actions he was considered equal to gods themselves.

There is a *sloka* regarding the history of astrology in the book *Brihatparasharhoshastra* written by sage Parashar around 700 A.D. It says:

Vishwasradnardo Vyaso Vashishthoatri Parasharah,
Lomasho Yavanah Suryashchyavanah Kashyapo Briguh
Pulastayo Manuracharyah Paulishah Shaunkoadigrah,
Gargo Marichirityate Gyeya Jyotipravartakah.

This *sloka* contains the names of all the savants who were connected with the science of Astrology. Bhrigu's name is included in it. This confirms that a learned person named Bhrigu did exist in the past who was an authority on astrology. Late Acharya Nemi Chandra Shastri, who was a renowned astrologer and author believed that Bhrigu lived around 100 A.D.

Whatever may be the case, it cannot be denied that Maharishi Bhrigu was a peer amongst the astrologers who had uncanny knowledge of the future. He cannot be compared to anyone else. His treatise *Bhrigu-Samhita* is a remarkable book. This book is full of such strange and unheard of terminology that it boggles the mind. Another special point is that most of the fortune-tellers in the world only predicted the future.

But, in *Bhrigu-Samhita*, not only the future, but the past and the present are also exhaustively detailed in equal measure.

Bhrigu-Samhita is the form of dialogue between Mahrishi Bhrigu and his son Acharya Shukra. Its style is similar to that of dialogues between Arjuna and Lord Krishna in *Gita*. Every time, Acharya Shukra puts the same question:

> Vad nath dayasindho janma-lagnashubhashubham,
> Yen vigyatmatrain trikalagyo bhavishyati.

The word 'drashet' occurs many times in this treatise. In Sanskrit this word is used to depict something that is seen or caused to be seen. This testifies that Bhrigu had the divine insight to see the past or peep into the future. Many pages in this book deal with the previous life of the subject. Attempt has also been made to explain the present problems and difficulties with reference to one's actions in the previous birth. At one place Acharya Shukra asks Maharishi Bhrigu:

> Purvajanmakritam papam keedrikchev tapobal,
> Tad vadasva dayasindho yen bhuyatrikalagya.

In most of the predictions, details are given of previous birth, present life and future birth as well. In certain places, it has been indicated that when, where and why a person would consult *Bhrigu-Samhita* and whether he would do so with faith in that book or disbelieve what it says about him. Many scholars have testified that details regarding one's wife have been correctly fore-told only on the basis of the horoscope of the husband and without referring to the wife's horoscope.

There is reference to the year, month and day when any one goes to have his future read in *Bhrigu-Samhita*. Some predictions are made on the basis of time of consulting the book. Sometimes the questioner finds that details regarding his place of birth, residence, the first letter of his name as well as his father's name are also mentioned. Places are referred to by their ancient names.

There are many references to things that could not be imagined in the past. The book refers to legislator, social, welfare, secretariat, judge, transfer, insurance, aeroplane, operation, X'ray and many other medical instruments, interview, Vice-chancellor, commerce, metal-detector, company, Magistrate, District Magistrate, Commissioner, salary, pension, heart attack, engineering, motor, two-wheeler, advocate and finance companies. These things are products of modern age. It is surprising that Bhrigu mentions them when they did not exist in his time.

34

Many people believe that Bhrigu was the greatest amongst astrologers.

A prosperous person went to a priest who possessed the book *Bhrigu-Samhita* with a journalist friend of mine. He was anxious to know about his future. He had businesses at many places. The pandit took out a page and read, "This person will be arraigned before a magistrate in 1976 for smuggling. In spite of all efforts to defend himself, he will be sentenced to a prison term. He will suffer from skin disease in the prison. At that time, my friend and that person made fun of the fortune-teller. Everybody was amazed when these predictions came to be true later.

There are many horoscopes in *Bhrigu-Samhita* in which an absolutely new word comes while unravelling the future. This new word is invariably expounded in great details. This is natural. If a thing did not exist at the time this book was written, then the writer had to explain it in an exhaustive manner.

India's horoscope has been dealt with in *Bhrigu-Samhita* in an exhaustive manner and the details cover some 200 pages. Many places are referred to with their names and future events have been seriously analysed.

Some people regard *Bhrigu-Samhita* as a book of 500-600 pages. For them this sloka is cited.

Pitravyashcha sukham purna naagtrishatshat kaveh,

Samyak brumi phalam tatra pitravyashcha mahattram.

The father and elder brother of the questioner will enjoy all comforts. Details are given on page 3,800. There are many *slokas* that refer to pages 3,900, 4,154 and even further pages. No body knows how many pages *Bhrigu-Samhita* contains.

In the year 1979, when I was not established in journalism and had never thought of writing books, I had shown my horoscope to a pandit at Allahabad. He drew up a picture of my future and it has proved correct till today. He predicted that my wife will be a liberal and I will have two daughters. I was shown my wife's horoscopes when I was not even married. At that time I thought that it was a ruse to fleece me of some money. I remember one *sloka* from my wife's horoscope:

Pustakana chaiv nirmata patishchasya bhavishyati

There were many prophesies hidden in this *sloka* and they have proved to be true. I had been told in 1979 that my father Pt. Yagya Datt Sharma will suffer from fractures in the legs in a road accident and in 1989 it has come to pass.

In view of the above, it can be safely asserted that no one has excelled Bhrigu *rishi* as a fore-caster of future and astrologer who could unravel the past as well as the future. ■ ■

Saratchandra and *Bhrigu-Samhita*

Saratchandra Chatterji, the great Bengali novelist and short story writer, had written a letter to his friend one Hari Das Chattopadhyay on April 7, 1920 from Shivala in Banaras. This letter has been reproduced in Bengali Book entitled 'Saratchandra Through the Mirror of his Characters'. It reads:

"I will tell you a very interesting thing. There is a pandit here who is famous for his Bhrigu-Samhita. *He looked into my horoscope and was bewildered and so was I. He told me about my past, which is hardly known to anyone till this day in such a correct manner that I had to hang my head in shame. The future is still more unnerving. He said that this horoscope belongs to some yogi or some person of royal lineage. I had kept my identity secret."*

Luca Gaurico: Fortune-teller *Par Excellence*

Luca Gaurico was considered as one of the most renowned and dependable fortune-tellers in his times. He possessed a natural gift for forecasting and had no parallel in making astrological calculations. He was a contemporary of the famous fortune-teller Nostradamus. He had a very shy nature and usually kept to himself. He made many prophesies out of which some forty proved to be absolutely correct. The rest remain to be verified in the times to come.

S aint Luca Gaurico had just come out after a bath. He was looking down from an oriel of his residence that a ball fell into his garden. A little later, a young boy entered the garden to pick up the ball. He picked up the ball and turned round to leave.

The saint gazed intently at the face of that boy. Suddenly he became agitated and ran towards the garden like an excited child. He was able to stop the boy before he could leave his garden. When the disciples of the saint saw this, they came running to the place. They saw that the eyes of the saint were glowing. He then announced in a resounding voice, "Those who are seeing this boy should greet him respectfully. One day, this young lad shall be elected as Pope.

And in 1513, this boy named Giovanni de Medici was really crowned as Pope Leo X. The saint's prediction had come to be true to the last letter. This incident belongs to the period, when another soothsayer Nostradamus must have been playing in his mother's lap. At that time, Gaurico was considered as the uncrowned king of all fortune-tellers.

Giovanni de Medici, who became Pope Leo X as prophesied by Luca Gaurico.

Gaurico possessed some natural gift insofar as predicting of the future was concerned. Apart from it, he had no parallel in making astronomical calculations. Once, he had predicted that a Pope would die in November 1954, and it may surprise the readers that Pope Paul III died in that month and year.

Gaurico is credited with making sixty predictions. The most famous of these predictions is the one he made when he was quite old and Nostradamus had already established his name in this line. Bologna was a city state in North Italy. It was under the despotic rule of Giovanni Bentivoglio. Bentivoglio was extremely superstitious and idiosyncratic. He once called Gaurico to his court to make predictions regarding him.

Gaurico took his seat on the floor in the court. After some time, he said, "I perceive that the king will lose his throne and die in exile. This is going to happen soon."

Bentivoglio was mad with rage on hearing this. He snatched a whip from the executioner and gave saint Luca fifteen lashes with it. Then he asked, "Now, tell me what the future holds for you.' Gaurico retained his composure even after his public humiliation. He stood there patiently and declared that he was not going to die at that time. Benti-

King Henry II of France lost his eyes and life in a duel forecast by Luca Gaurico.

voglio took out a sword and rushed to strike him when the other courtiers prevented him from doing so.

Luca Gaurico's name shall always top the list of fortune-tellers who always tell the truth without fear. Once the crown princess Catherine of France called him and asked him to tell her the destiny of her fiancee Prince Henry. Gaurico unhesitatingly told her, "When Henry ascends the throne, in the very first year there shall be blood bath in the court. Two princes will fight a duel in which one shall lose his life. Henry will be engaged in such a duel after he becomes Emperor. In this duel, he shall become blind and will die a tragic death due to injuries sustained in the head."

After some time, when Henry ascended the throne as the new Emperor, Gaurico's first prediction came to be true in an amazing manner on July 10, 1547. Guy Chabot de Jarnac and Francois de Vivonne Chataignerie exchanged angry words on some trivial matter. Suddenly they started fighting a duel without even caring for the presence of the Emperor. Before the fight could be stopped, Jarnac had killed Chataignerie.

Catherine became worried from that day. The first part of Gaurico's prediction had been fulfilled. She invited the young fortune-teller Nostradamus to Paris, keeping it as a secret. After a strenuous journey of one month, Nostradamus reached the palace. He also said the same thing

39

which Gaurico had already predicted. But, he said it in a roundabout and ambiguous manner. The Queen asked Nostradamus regarding Gaurico's prediction about the Emperor, Nostradamus gave a clever and double meaning answer. He said, "If the Emperor does not take part in a duel, how can the prediction be fulfilled."

By July, 1559, Emperor Henry had forgotten that he should not indulge in any fight or duel. He covered his body with armour and wore a gold studded helmet. Then, he invited Montgomery, the chief of his guards, for a duel with spears. In no time, had Montgomery's spear pierced the eyes of the Emperor. During the beginning of August, Emperor Henry died a painful death due to infection of injuries in the head. After all, he could not escape the future written for him by the powerful finger of destiny.

Gaurico had predicted the emergence of a powerful gang of criminals in Italy. This gang was to be known as La Cosa Nostra. He predicted that this gang will be dreaded in the entire world for organised crimes on large scale. This prediction also came to be absolutely correct when the Mafia organisation took birth in 1869. The Italian translation of Mafia is La Cosa Nostra. This organisation has made entry into all the sections of society. These groups are notorious for organised killings, smuggling and other heinous crimes. In many countries, Mafia is able to influence government decisions at the highest level. In common parlance the word Mafia has become synonymous with organised group of bad characters and criminals. ■ ■

Peter Harkos

The name of Peter Harkos had hit newspaper headlines many a time because of his uncanny gift of divine insight. Peter works for Dutch intelligence. It is said that once he fell from a great height. After the accident, he felt that he had developed a sort of sixth sense. He could tell the position of a questioner by simply hearing his voice. Not only that, he could sense his problems without being told about them. By only touching a thing, he is able to tell extraordinary details about it. He says that he is able to do so by concentrating on it.

Mother Shipton: Fortune-teller Nonpareil

If there was any fortune-teller that could be compared with Nostradamus, the renowned French forecaster, it was Mother Shipton alias Ursula Sontheil of England. This deformed woman who has correctly predicted many earth-shaking events is considered by some as ahead of the great Nostradamus himself. Unlike Nostradamus, her predictions were precise and unambiguous. She came on the scene earlier than Nostradamus and some people believe that Nostradamus has repeated, after a lapse of fifty years, what she had already predicted in the first half of the sixteenth century. Let us recapitulate some of her astounding predictions.

S he was born as Ursula Sontheil in July, 1488, in the town of Knaresbrough in Yorkshire in England. She was a handicapped child and hence was considered accursed in those times. Her childhood was spent in an orphanage. Her body looked like a dehydrated corpse, crooked legs and hands together with portruding eyes made her a hideous sight. Her nose resembled the snout of some animal. Nobody liked Ursula because of her ugliness.

Her primary education was provided by church. Because of her appearance, the other children teased her. But, Ursula had inner mental strength. She used it to punish the children who tormented her. Soon, she was removed from the school. It is said that the capacity to foresee the future developed in her during her days at the orphanage.

No authoritative details are available regarding her transformation into Mother Shipton from Ursula Sontheil. It is certain that she was

Mother Shipton

Mother Shipton was the first to predict the execution of Charles I.

married to one Toby Shipton at the age of twenty two. Toby belonged to York. After her marriage to Toby, his friends came to know about her capacity to predict future. A number of people were at her doors to know their future. Till the age of 25, Ursula did not make any remarkable predictions. Her prophesies were confined to mundane matters like sex of the expected child, time of marriage, health problems, results in examinations and other such routine affairs.

Her first important prophesy after being christened Mother Shipton was: "When the English lion sets foot on the Gaelic shore, the lily flowers would just wither away. The women of the country of lilies will shed copious tears. The royal eagle will side with the English lion and together they shall subdue their opponents."

The above prophesy seems like an allegorical tale. It turned out to be true in the year 1513. Henry VIII, King of England anchored with 50,000 troops on the Gaelic shore. The national flower of France is lily. The French were pale with fear at the thought of such a big attack on their country. The Roman Emperor Maximillian was well known as royal

Shipton had prophesied regarding the troubles of common people and liquidation of monasteries during the reign of Henry VIII.

Mother Shipton had also predicted the fall of the great Cardinal Wolsey.

eagle. He came to help the English and Henry won a great victory. The women of France must have shed a lot of tears on account of loss of husbands, brothers and sons in the battle.

Another of her famous predictions was one made in 1546, which has come to be true in the modern age. She said, "A time will come soon when human beings will travel upon and under the water. Steel shall float on water."

She had also predicted, "Many nations will come together to form an association. It will provide solutions to problems and show the way to nations." The League of Nations and United Nations Organisation had been envisaged by her in the 16th century.

In another prophesy, she said, "First they shall invent bombs that will cause widespread destruction. These bombs will spread rays of death and diseases. Then they will sit together and think of ways to destroy them. Strange would be the ways of the rulers in future. Many systems of governments will prevail and they will undergo frequent changes." Isn't amazing that she could foresee atomic and hydrogen bombs, chemical weapons and germ warfare. Not only that she had also hinted about different forms of governments that prevail in the present times — from monarchy to democracy, dictatorship and communist states, which

Roman Emperor, Maximillian, also known as 'Royal Eagle'. Henry won a great victory in 1513 with his assistance.

have been indulging in constant struggles and cold war. There is no doubt that she had amazing power to discern the future.

Mother Shipton is credited with some 400 prophesies. She had predicted about the downfall of Cardinal Wolsey. She had foretold regarding the troubles of common men during the reign of Emperor Henry. She also said that the power of church would decline and that the monasteries would be liquidated. Another famous prophesy was regarding the beheading of King Charles I of England. Many other astrologers had predicted about the killing of Charles I, but she was the first to make it. She had said:-

The white king shall wear the crown
And will have Lily as his wife,
But soon the sword of an executioner,
Will deprive him of his dear life.

The meaning of this prophesy is crystal clear. Charles I had married Princess Henerietta Maria of France. She was lovingly called Lily. The King wore white gown at the time of his coronation, and was, as everybody knows, executed by the people.

Another prophesy of Mother Shipton:
A day shall soon come
When coaches will run without horses,
There shall be many accidents on the roads,
And people will be greatly worried.

She had foreseen the congestion on the roads due to petrol driven vehicles and the resultant increase in road accidents that would cause widespread anxiety and sorrow.

The genius of Mother Shipton was acknowledged when Sir Walter Raleigh brought the plants of potato and tobacco.

In one of her astounding prophesies, she had said that the time is not far when thoughts and words shall reach all the corners of the world before one could wink twice. It indicated that she could visualise the advent of wireless, telegraph, radio, teleprinter, telephone, telex and television at some future date. These things are commonplace nowadays, but in her time they could only be distant and exotic dreams.

She had also made a prophesy about the great adventurer, Walter Raleigh. She said he will cross many seas and bring back with him plants with roots and big leaves. The first will be staple food and the other will be used as intoxicant. Walter Raleigh had brought plants of potato and tobacco. The one is staple food all over the world and the other led to the manufacturing of cigarettes which provide smoking pleasure to many.

She had even predicted in 1650 that she would die next year at the age of 73. ■■

Vanga Dimitrova

Vanga Dimitrova is a blind fortune teller of Bulgaria. So many people crowded at her place to know their future that the government had to pass a Dimitrova Security Act in 1965. Now, a committee first examines the questions to be sent to her. It is only then that she replies to suitable queries. The Government of Bulgaria pays her a monthly salary and charges fees from the people who consult her regarding the future.

Dimitrova generally predicts about personal matters, but they are invariably correct.

Nostradamus: Prophetic Fortune-teller

Considered as an institution in himself, Nostradamus is the only person to have made more than 3000 prophesies. There has been no forecaster in the history of mankind who could see so far ahead as Nostradamus. It is said that half of his prophesies have proved to be true. The other half are still to be tested as he has made prophesies regarding events up to the year 3797 A.D. He seemed to have a remarkable control over the science of forecasting as he could feel and sense the coming events hundreds of years before they were supposed to happen. He thought more and talked less. He led a rigorous life as a pious Roman Catholic and distributed most of his income to the poor. Most of his prophesies could be placed into the category of premonitions.

The French Revolution was at its peak. It was the month of May. Three idiocyncratic persons were busy in digging a grave. On the head-stone of the grave was inscribed, "Anyone who tried to remove my body from this place will be killed instantaneously." The three ignored the warning.

It was the grave of the greatest forecaster of the future, namely Michel de Nostradamus. It was widely held that if anyone drank wine in his skull, he would be as famous a fortune-teller as the man in that grave. But the warning inscribed on the grave deterred people from trying to disturb his grave.

46

The grave was dug before midnight. Only one amongst the three grave diggers could gather enough courage to peep at the skeleton of Nostradamus in the coffin. He thought for some time and then severed the skull from the skeleton. He took out a bottle of champagne from the pocket of his trousers and poured the wine into the skull.

The wine started oozing out of the open eyes of the skull. That man lifted the skull to his mouth holding it fast with both the hands. He started gulping the wine rapidly. He had hardly taken four sips that a stray bullet hit him in the neck and he fell down dead. The revolutionaries might have fired a bullet at someone and it struck this man.

The other two took to their heels. They turned round once to have a look at the skeleton. A copper plate was lying on the chest of the skeleton. The letters engraved on the plate were glowing in that darkness. They read — May 1793 ... It is apparent that Nostradamus must have got this plate engraved before his death with the month and year of this incident which he could clearly foresee.

Verily, he had the prophetic vision to see the future. He was not born with this gift. Michel de Nostradamus was born in a Jewish family on December 14, 1503 in the afternoon. His maternal grandfather, Jean de Saint Remy, was a renowned physician and astrologer. He instructed Michel about herbs of different kinds and asked him to develop interest in the matter. When his maternal grandfather died after some time, the entire trend of his education was changed. His father got him admitted to Montpellier University to study medicine. Soon, Nostradamus was busy in fighting the epidemic of plague that smote the country. He earned a good name as a successful doctor. A little after, he got married in 1533. Soon, plague again broke out and his wife and child died. These shocking deaths nearly broke his heart. For eight long years, Nostradamus wandered through France, Italy and Sicily.

His reputation as a forecaster was established during the time he was staying in Lorraine with his friend Seigneur de Florinville. He had gone there to treat the mother of his friend of some ailment.

Florinville did not believe in destiny and used to make fun of Nostradamus on this account. He was always on the lookout for a pretext to tease Nostradamus. One day, both the friends were walking in the morning. When they reached the backyard of the house, Florinville pointed out two pigs to Nostradamus. One was black and another white. He asked Nostradamus to predict about the future of the pigs.

47

The great Nostradamus. It is believed that none of his prophesies has proved incorrect to this day.

Nostradamus knew that his friend was pulling his legs. Even then, he calmly predicted, "The white pig would be eaten up by a dog tonight." Florinville made fun of this prediction and called upon his servants to serve the white pig's meat for dinner that night.

A lot of respectable people were seated at the dining table that night. When pig's meat was served, Florinville teasingly asked Nostradamus, "Friend, what are we eating?"

Nostradamus calmly replied, "The meat of the black pig."

Florinville immediately made enquiries from his wife and cook in this respect. They told him that it was the meat of the black pig. The reason being that when the meat of white pig was cut and placed on a table, the dogs had rendered it unsuitable for the guests by eating some portion out of it. Hence, the black pig had to be killed and cooked.

Nostradamus made very few prophesies till 1547. He did it occasionally. His interest lay in interpreting the zodiac signs and telling

Nostradamus had already predicted mass annihilation due to powerful bombs.

people their annual forecast. Apart from that, he took keen interest in treating people and was rewarded many times for his success in curing people.

It was during this period that he married Anne Ponsart Gamelle, a widow, and decided to spend the rest of his life in the town of Salon. He also wrote a book about enhancing beauty, increasing sexual powers, manufacture of cosmetics, retaining youth and making pickles and jams. This book was published in the year 1552 under the title 'Traite des Fardemens'.

Nostradamus was a short statured man. His height was only 5'3", and he never slept for more than four hours a day. He was a quiet man, who talked very little but thought more. He was a strict Roman Catholic and used to fast for two days in a week. He also distributed most of his income amongst the poor.

Nostradamus' favourite disciple was one Jean Aimes de Chavigny. Chavigny remained with him till the end of his life. According to him, Nostradamus started developing the inner powers after reading 'Mysteriis Egyptorum', a book on Egyptian occult science of charms and incantations. Nostradamus demonstrated these powers many times.

Nostradamus wrote his book 'Centuries' to predict about the coming events. It took him four years to write this book. It was published on May 4, 1555. People stood in a queue before Mace Bonhomme Press to buy a copy. There was a tremendous demand for the book. The first edition was sold on the day the book came out of the Press. This book contains predictions from the time of Nostradamus to the time when the entire world will be annihilated. The people were greatly disappointed when they failed to comprehend its language. Many versions of 'Centuries' were brought out by 1558. Many learned authors brought out this book in a simplified version and language.

In the beginning of the book, Nostradamus had given a mysterious message to his newly born son. The message is in the form of a letter. It said that it is useless to take interest in forecasting future. It may prove detrimental. When his son Caesar attained the age of 22, he thought of taking advantage of his father's reputation by making predictions. He did not pay any attention to the message warning him against indulging in this profession which was the purport of the letter. He paid a heavy price for ignoring it.

He predicted that the city of Vivarais would be reduced to cinders. Vivarais was at that time under the occupation of royal forces. When

Nostradamus had definitely hinted about the ascension of Elizabeth to the throne of England.

50

nothing happened for some time, people again asked Caesar, "When will Vivarais be destroyed." Unhesitatingly Caesar answered, "Within three days." The next night, the soldiers caught hold of Caesar and killed him. He was trying to start a fire in the city.

Nostradamus has not mentioned dates regarding his prophesies in the book 'Centuries'. He has given the reason in the beginning of the book. He has said, "I do not want my contemporaries to suffer from any controversy or tyranny because of my premonitions regarding the coming ages. It is for this reason that I have used a difficult and mysterious language."

In many matters, Nostradamus has indicated firm dates regarding the events. He has written, "The year 1792 shall be of special significance to France. The common man shall inherit the government, he will become strong and a new age will be ushered in." Everybody knows that it turned out to be the year of French Revolution, when the monarchy was overthrown. The French revolutionaries had occupied the palace and the revolutionary slogan of 'equality, liberty and fraternity' rent the air.

Centuries contains predictions up to the year 3797. There are many astronomical calculations in this book. Most of its predictions are in the form of premonitions of its author. The strange thing is that the riddle like language of the book may seem incomprehensible before the

The Great London Fire, predicted by Nostradamus.

51

Queen Catherine de Medici of France, whose husband Henry II of France died in a duel.

event, but after the event, the language becomes crystal clear and is easily understood. Many examples can be cited to prove this.

A forecast regarding the royal family of France runs like this. "The young lion shall subdue the old one. In a warlike situation, he will blind him in a golden cage. He will die a tragic death after receiving two injuries."

The purport of this prediction becomes crystal clear after the event. In July, 1559, two marriages took place in the French royal family. Celebrations were held for three days in Paris. Emperor Henry took part in these celebrations with great enthusiasm. He invited the commander of Scottish soldiers, Montgomery, to have a duel with him with spears. It was to be fought on horseback. The person who was able to dehorse the other with the spear was to be declared the winner.

Captain Montgomery was only 23 years of age at that time, while Henry was in his forty second year. Both wore lion-shape d armour so that they are not hurt, as it was a friendly duel. Montgomery cleverly attacked Henry in the first round. Henry got tired, and when Montgomery attacked him with his spear in the second round, he could not take evasive defence. The spear pierced his neck and got entangled in his helmet. There was an immediate uproar. Henry's armour was taken off. It was found that he had lost an eye. He died after ten days in a painful state due to the two injuries in the eye and the neck.

Nostradamus has made many correct predictions about the French royal family and other princely families. Nostradamus had predicted a

The young Napolean.
Nostradamus had correctly
predicted his rise and fall.

long time ago, regarding the children of Emperor Henry and Queen Catherine de Medici. He had prophesied, "Their son Francis will be married to Mary, Queen of Scots, and he will die before he completes one year of his reign. The younger sister of Francis, Princess Elizabeth will be married to Philip, the aged Emperor of Spain. She will be a child-bride and will also die very young. The second Princess Claude will die before she completes thirteen years of her age. The other two younger Princes, Charles and Henry, will become Emperors of France and Poland. Henry would be later assassinated."

Nostradamus has written this regarding Queen Elizabeth I of England. "One, who has been cast away and wronged will ascend the throne one day. Her enemies would be treated as traitors. She will reign for a long period and it shall be glorious. She will die at the age of 70 when it will be the third year." This riddle like forecast becomes clear when we find that the neglected Princess Elizabeth ascended the throne of England. Her reign is supposed to be a golden period in British history. When she died at the age of 70, the year was 1603, the third year of the new century.

Nostradamus has referred to England as Britain at many places. Readers must be aware that the name Britain was thought of hundreds of years after Nostradamus. In an interesting prophesy he has said, "The Senate in London would sentence the King to death." And verily, King Charles I was sentenced to death publicly. It could not even be imagined in Nostradamus' time. Nostradamus had also correctly predicted the 'Great Plague' and 'Great Fire', in London. These two events took place in exactly the same manner as he had envisaged.

He had successfully guessed the naval war between England and Netherland in the years 1665-1667. It was a very fierce battle. Nostradamus had predicted that King Edward VIII of England will abdicate the throne to marry a woman of his choice. He had also said that the shy and lazy Prince of York will be crowned King as George VI.

Nostradamus had made correct guesses about the rise and fall of Napoleon and Hitler. According to his predictions, a dictator will emerge

Edward VIII of England, who abdicated the crown to marry Wally Simpson (sitting alongside).

Nostradamus and India

It is amazing that Nostradamus, who lived some 400 years ago, correctly predicted about events that were to happen in the next 3,000 years. In the 74th quatrain of the sixth section of his book 'Centuries', he has written:-

"The most powerful woman of the land surrounded by sea on three sides will regain her position due to disunity amongst her opponents. She will be killed by her own security guards in her own house before completing 67 years of her age. This shall occur when there would be sixteen years to go before the advent of the new century." We need not emphasise that Nostradamus had predicted the future of Mrs. Indira Gandhi who was assassinated in the year 1984, sixteen years before the advent of 21st century.

Nostradamus presumes the following in the 75th quatrain of the tenth section. "The new century will begin after the use of weapons of mass annihilation which shall decimate humanity. A Hindu leader will then show the new way to the world.

The most important prophesies that Nostradamus has made regarding India are as follows: "The world war shall start after the Mongols use weapons that disseminate rays of death. The war will take a new turn due to India's friendship with two most powerful countries in the world. The war shall end in the fifth year of the new century; that is, peace will be established in 2006. Europe will abjure its religion and accept the oldest religion in the world. 75% of the humanity will be destroyed in this war. A spiritual leader from South India will guide the world."

No one knows, if these predictions of Nostradamus would be fulfilled and prove to be correct as has his 2500 other prophesies.

amongst the Arabs who will bring the world to the brink of a world war. The great powers will unitedly oppose him. Maybe, he referred to the present crisis in the Gulf countries created by the occupation of Kuwait by the forces of Saddam Hussein, dictator of Iraq. We find all the great powers, America, Russia, Britain, France and China raged against him.

At one place Nostradamus has written, "The King of terror will descend from the sky in the seventh month of the year 1999." Continuing this prophesy he has further added that this originator of terror will be clad in a blue turban and gown. For 27 years he would terrorise the world. There are still many years left for this prophesy to be tested on the touchstone of truth.

55

If a close study is made of the prophesies made by Nostradamus one would find that he had foreseen the atomic attacks on Hiroshima and Nagasaki. He has written, "Deadly fire shall spread automatically. These bombs shall cause large scale deaths and destruction."

There are many other prophesies of Nostradamus the correctness of which is yet to be verified. Because of his genius as well as the correctness of hundreds of his prophesies, it is presumed that the rest of them will also prove to be true. After all, a man who could predict about the death sentence on the French Emperor and Empress, rise and fall of Napoleon together with all his military campaigns, advent and decline of Hitler and many such things in the coming centuries, could never be wrong. This view is held all over the world.

Nostradamus could also foresee his death. He had prophesied, "When I would have safely kept the gift of the Emperor on return from the embassy, I would not have to work any longer. I would meet my creator. My friends, brothers and close associates will find my dead body between the bed and a bench."

On July 1, 1566, Nostradamus called a priest and made confession of his sins. In the evening he called his favourite disciple Chavigny and calmly told him, "My time is up. I shall not be alive tomorrow morning."

Chavigny was unnerved. He paced outside the room of Nostradamus till late in the night. Getting tired, he went to sleep in a corner. He woke up in the morning. He found the dead body of Nostradamus lying upside down between his bed and a stool. He had left for his heavenly abode. ■ ■

Madame Blavatsky

Madame Blavatsky

A Russian woman, Helena Petrova Hahn, has earned a name in the field of forecasting. Born in a royal family, Madame Blavatsky could predict future of the people by simply having a look at them. She had studied occult science in Egypt in 1851. She came to India many times after the 1857 War of Independence. She founded the Theosophist Society in this country. She died in England on May 8, 1891. By then she had been charged with offences like deception, fraud and hypocrisy. No important prophesy made by her is available.

Dr. John Dee : The Original Agent 007

He was supposed to be an accomplished forecaster, tantrik and an enlightened person. His tragedy was that he could never prove that he was not lying. Some people including Queen Elizabeth I thought him to be divine person, who could look beyond the present and correctly peep into the future. On the other hand, a large number of people looked upon him as a hypocrite, swindler and a cunning person. The reality is unknown, but this is certain that he was a learned person whose knowledge of astronomy was deep and authoritative.

When he died in 1608, very few people knew about John Dee. Perhaps, he himself did not know that he would die unknown and unsung. But, at one time he was the favourite of Queen Elizabeth I of England, who had great respect for him and had appointed him as her personal astrologer.

She owed him a great debt of gratitude. He had brought her out of her depression by forecasting, "Do not despair, as the gods have indicated to me that you shall become the Queen in another four months."

Elizabeth I could not forget this prediction as well as the man who had made it, after ascending the throne of England. The man who predicted her ascension was a bearded old man, who wore loose clothes and was very ordinary looking . He was also referred to as a doctor.

Exactly four months after in 1558, Mary Tudor, Queen of England died. She was succeeded by her half-sister Elizabeth and as such the prophesy of the old doctor turned out to be true. To show her gratitude,

Though Dr. John Dee made many correct predictions, he is supposed to be an incomplete fortune-teller.

Elizabeth issued an order, "Dr. John Dee is appointed as our personal astrologer," as soon as she was crowned Queen of England.

It is supposed that from that very moment, efforts were initiated to undermine his position. That was natural as court intrigues were a constant feature of those times.

John was born in a poor family on July 13, 1527, in Mortlake near London. His father was a poor and ignorant villager, John was interested in studies from his childhood. He was quite talented. He entered Cambridge University at the age of fifteen. At 20, he was already a Fellow of the famed Trinity College.

John had great interest in astronomical calculations from the very beginning. He travelled throughout Europe and gave lectures at many places. His reputation soared high and it was said that he had no parallel in astronomy and in the study of the stars in his time.

It was only in 1554 that John fearlessly made a public forecast. He said, "The reign of Queen Mary shall come to an end in four years." At that time the repression let loose by Mary Tudor was at its peak. Readers may recall that this fanatical Queen had unleashed terror on the Protestants. They were being burnt on stake. John Dee was immediately arrested for predicting the above. He was sent up for trial and many irrelevant charges were framed against him. He was released in 1555. As

58

John Dee became famous for his prophesy regarding death of Mary Tudor.

he came out of the prison, John Dee started pursuing vigorously the career of a fortune-teller.

It was after some time of his release that he wrote a letter to Princes Elizabeth, who was interned. He wrote, "From the study of the horoscope of Queen Mary Tudor I can say that her reign of terror is coming to an end, as she shall die soon. I shall send you some special information in this connection at an early date."

This letter fell into the hands of the spies of Queen Mary Tudor. John Dee was arraigned in the court on charges of treason, black magic and conspiracy to kill the Queen. For reasons unknown the court proceedings were abruptly dropped. It remains an unsolved mystery. John Dee then engaged himself in the task of fortune-telling. Till the death of Mary Tudor, he remained in the background and made small prophesies.

The importance and position of John Dee underwent a remarkable change as Elizabeth ascended the throne of England. Apart from appointing him as her court astrologer, she entrusted him with the task of spying in the courts of foreign rulers. He was given the code name of 007. Inspired by this, Ian Fleming gave the same name to his fictitious spy James Bond.

Dr. Dee started experimenting with corpses dug out of their graves in the year 1581. He thought that he could get the help of spirits in divulging the future. He was caught in this act in 1582, but as he was a favourite of the Queen, nothing could be initiated against him.

It was during one such experiment with the dead that he prophesied on May 5, 1583, that England would be attacked by a foreign power from the sea and that the Queen of Scotland would be sentenced to death. It may be a coincidence or good luck, both these prophesies proved to be correct and the reputation of John Dee was now at its peak.

In his work of contacting the spirits, John Dee was assisted by a person named Edward Kelly. He used to act as a medium between the

Standing in a consecrated circle, John Dee and Edward Kelly talking to a spirit.

60

Edward Kelly, the
medium between spirits
and John Dee.

spirits and John Dee. Somehow, he got angry with Dee and left him in 1587.

After this, John Dee withdrew himself into his own world. His work also declined. He always claimed that he he could talk to the gods and spirits. Now, suddenly he assumed silence. When he died in 1608, very few people were aware of his name and work.

There are many books available on the life and prophesies of John Dee. The modern astrologers and learned persons do not place any importance on his prophesies. It is supposed that he was only a half-baked forecaster who could not improve his capacity and talents.

A Temple of Atonement

There is a memorial built in the memory of Emperor Fya Kong. This monument is located in the state of Nacorn in the Pathom area of Thailand. This monument reminds one of a prophesy.

Fya Kong had only one son. When his son Farn was born, the astrologers advised the King to either kill the new born prince or exile him. They thought that the lines of his hand indicated that he would one day kill his father.

Fya Kong immediately exiled Prince Farn. After a long time, they came face to face with each other. As luck would have it, they were pitted against each other in a duel. Farn killed his father. Later, when he learnt that he had committed the sin of patricide, he was struck with remorse. He then built a memorial to his father in the shape of a large temple. It still exists there.

61

Kenneth Mackenzie: The Saint of Brahan

His predictions were correct and premonitions to the point. People preferred to call him as the Seer of Brahan rather than by his name. Most of the astrologers of the past have used a riddle like language in their predictions making them complex for the ordinary people. It was Kenneth Mackenzie's speciality that he predicted about persons, families, royal personages, cities, rivers and inventions in an easy to comprehend and direct language. You do not have to deal with mind boggling and ambiguous style. It is amazing that everything that he forecast has come out to be absolutely true. We give below a few of his astounding predictions that have stood the test of time.

"The strenuous climb to the high mountains shall be smooth. The road to the heights will be like a ribbon and coaches driven by machines will move about in the valleys. The valleys themselves will be joined by metal bridges."

"The drinking water shall reach the houses and food will be cooked by the fire that would flow into each house."

"Coaches connected to each other will run on iron rails and will make thousands of people at one time from one place to another. They will not be driven by animals but by human brains."

"Ships will travel deep inside the oceans and will attack the enemy with arrows of fire."

Sir Walter Scott believed that the people of Scotland possessed sixth sense.

The man who made such clear and unambiguous predictions was named Kenneth Mackenzie. He is also remembered as Coinneach Fiosaiche or Seer of Brahan. He is supposed to have been born either at the end of 16th century or the beginning of the 17th century. No details are available regarding the exact year of his birth. Authoritative details are of course available about his death. Kenneth had been burnt alive. He was charged with divulging in public the secret and personal matters of the royal family and insulting the members of the royal family. Another charge was that he followed the devil's path.

The Seer of Brahan had said this regarding his death, "Two birds will come from two directions after my body is reduced to ashes. One shall be a swan and another a crow. They will hover over my ashes for some time and then go away. The place shall become a memorial but those who have ordered my death shall have no member of their family alive. Their entire dynasty will be finished."

And this is what exactly happened. We shall come to it later. We shall now examine the predictions made by the Seer of Brahan which have enhanced his reputation to such heights.

The people inhabiting the highlands in Scotland have what is known as 'sixth sense'. Practically everyone there has the hidden and un-developed capacity for premonitions regarding future events. There are many proofs for the above statement. The famous writer, Sir Walter

Scott, had written many articles that prove that these people have a natural gift of sixth sense.

The Seer of Brahan had a mysterious stone. He could see the future in this blue coloured precious stone. There are many stories making the rounds in Scotland as to how he came into the possession of this stone or gem.

This fortune-teller started making predictions to earn his living. His calculations were so exact and predictions so correct that his name spread far and wide. People looked upon him as someone gifted with inner sight and started referring to him as the Seer of Brahan.

One of his famous predictions was one that he made about the Caledonian Canal some hundred years before it was made. He had foretold, "Ships will ply behind the Tomnahaurich hill, from East to West and from West to East."

The Seer of Brahan had to say this regarding the fashion at the present time in England. He said, "The country will progress a lot. The youths will degenerate to a level that they would seem to be effeminate. They shall lack courage to this extent that a flock of sheep will be enough to cause fear in them."

He once predicted in such a way that it seems that he had occult powers and he was a very enlightened person. Mackenzie of Lokalch misbehaved with him and in anger he cursed him, "Your entire wealth will be destroyed. It will be after a long time that Matheson, who shall be your descendant after many generations, will become its owner. The same thing happened. After some 128 years Alexander Matheson became its last inheritor.

He had also made a similar prediction regarding the Fairburn family. He told them that their palatial house will be ruined. Straw would be kept in the top floor room. A pregnant cow will reach it, eating the hay scattered on the steps. She will give birth to a calf. When this prediction was fulfilled, the newspapers splashed it prominently. This incident took place in 1870, when the Seer of Brahan had been dead for nearly 150 years.

The Seer of Brahan had made some 75 predictions regarding prominent persons and families. One amongst them is quoted, "When the bridge on Ness river slowly collapses, a lot of people would be on it. Amongst them would be one Mathew on a white horse accompanied by a pregnant woman. They will come to no harm as they would be at the other end of the bridge."

This came to be true. Only Mathew Campbell and a woman escaped in this disaster that took place in 1849. The records do not testify to the fact whether Mathew was on a white horse at that time. It is also not certain if the woman that accompanied him was pregnant or not.

The idea regarding the revolt at Culloden had flashed into the mind of the Seer of Brahan rather suddenly. He was passing through the area that he proclaimed, "After a few generations, there would be a bloody war here. Heads will roll from the bodies as ripe fruits fall from a tree during a storm. The land will be red with blood."

The third Earl of Seaforth, husband of Isabella, who had great faith in Coinneach.

Isabella, who got the Seer of Brahan killed so that he could not reveal facts regarding her life.

The saint of Brahan has mentioned about the exodus from the villages to the cities. He predicted that there would be shopping and commercial complexes on highways and ports will undergo unimaginable development. He even, describes the diseases caused by noise pollution. In one prediction, he had imagined an atomic submarine. He said, "There would be closed boats at Holy Loch. They would look like cows without legs and horns. These boats will be capable of firing flaming arrows that would release rays that shall cause death on a large scale." Nowadays, a submarine base is located near Holy Loch.

It is strange that his most remarkable act became the cause of his own death. The Earl of Seaforth had gone to Paris. His wife Isabella requested him to tell her about him. This is what he told her, "A pretty woman is the reason of his not returning. At this time, he is kneeling before her and begging for her love." Isabella forced out full details regarding the Earl's amorous adventures. The Seer of Brahan told her everything what was happening between that woman and the Earl in Paris. It must have been confirmed later.

Isabella became nervous and afraid of the remarkable capacity of Mackenzie. She thought that the Seer may tell the Earl about her own misdoings and lecherous life. She decided to do away with the Seer of Brahan. Then, he had related the romantic escapades of the Earl before a lot of people.

The Seer could gauge the thoughts of Isabella as he said this as soon as she left, "If anyone liquidates me, his entire dynasty would be wiped out. I know what is going to happen to me and the people who would put me to death. The last person of their family would be deaf and dumb. He shall have four sons. But no body from this family will rule over Brahan. All the property and lands will pass into the hands of a stranger."

Isabella flew into a rage when she learnt of this prophesy through her spies. She immediately ordered that the Seer of Brahan or Coinneach be taken to Channory Point and burnt alive.

Channory Point, where the Seer of Brahan was burnt alive. Swans can still be seen hovering over the spot.

When Coinneach was being taken to be burnt alive, Isabella shouted, "Foolish hypocrite, you have spoken so many lies that you shall rot in the hell."

The Seer of Brahan was held tight with ropes. He laughed. He pointed towards the sky and said, "I am not the only person ordained to die. People have died like this before and would be killed in the future. But, people who are put to death like this shall go to heaven, while you and your family will find place only in hell."

He further declared, "After my death when my ashes become cool, a swan and a crow will come here and hover round this place. If the swan sits on my ashes, I shall go to heaven. If the crow comes first and sits on my ashes, I shall go to hell."

The Seer was hung up upside down in a barrel full of fire on Isabella's signal. There were sharp iron rods under him that pierced his skull. Gradually he was reduced to cinders.

It is said that the Earl returned from his travels as the Seer was being put to death. He rushed to Channory Point to save him, but by that time Mackenzie had merged into the elements. It is said that the Earl stopped there and himself saw that a swan approached from the skies and sat on the Seer's ashes. Later on, a crow also came there. Recorded details are available regarding this remarkable incident.

The prophesy that the Seer of Brahan had made regarding the family of Isabella was fulfilled in 1794. The last male member of this family Earl Francis Humberston Mackenzie was not born deaf and dumb. He lost his power to hear and speak in an accident at the age of 12. He had four sons. But they all died before him. Humberston died on January 11, 1815.

The entire property was inherited by his daughter. She was a widow at that time. She remarried a person named Steward. Thus, as per the prophesy, a stranger became owner of the entire property and gradually this property was dissipated.

The Seer of Brahan had cursed that the Earl's daughter would be responsible for the death of her sister. One day, when both the sisters were travelling in a coach, they started quarreling. Mrs. Mackenzie flew into a temper and started whipping the horses. After a little while, the horses became out of control and the coach was upturned. The younger sister Caroline died in the accident.

In 1821, James Steward Mackenzie was declared as Baron of the Brahan-Seaforth area, but after two years, he died issueless. In this way, the entire family was finished as per prophesy of the Seer of Brahan.

■ ■

✽ Kozin ✽

Incidents regarding the time when the Russian forces were fighting in Italy in eighteenth century, are recorded in Russian history. A platoon of soldiers under the command of Captain Lukov lost its way in a blizzard. It so happened that the Russian soldiers had displayed exemplary bravery under Field Marshal Alexander Suvarov in the face of fierce bombardment from the fort of Turin. Major Pronin suggested that the area be surveyed before the troops advance any further.

During nightfall, a platoon of soldiers advanced through the bombardment. While returning, a snowstorm made it impossible for the soldiers to find the way. They would not see anything. Suddenly, a soldier shouted, "I can see. There is light ahead. Our soldiers are there."

He was an ordinary soldier named Kozin. The entire platoon was led by him to the camp of Suvarov. It was only then that the soldiers realised that Kozin had lost his eyes in mortar fire. His entire face was scorched and his eyes were only empty holes.

Who directed Kozin in that blizzard to find the way? It shall always remain a mystery.

Cagliostro: Genuine or Fraud ?

His was an enigmatic personality, it is difficult to assess whether he was a fraud or had genuine capacity to foretell future events. He tried his hands at many things. He indulged in black magic and wished to control ghosts and spirits. Making false prophesies, defrauding people and changing names were his forte. Some of his prophesies were astounding as they came to be true, but at the same time, he was christened as peer amongst cheats. If he had watched his steps and kept to honest and genuine predictions, he would have carved a place for himself. But, by nature he was a wily person after easy money. Destiny caught with him in the end and he had to spend his last days in a prison.

"Will I be able to see my future in this magic mirror?" enquired Madame Dubarry in an anxious tone.

"Definitely, you will see it in this mirror," Cagliostro replied confidently.

The beloved mistress of the Emperor of France, moved forward and peeped into the mirror. Her eyes widened with terror and her complexion turned pale at what she saw in that mirror. "Oh, no.........never" she exclaimed and became unconscious.

Nobody knew at that time as to what this woman saw in the mirror. She regained composure after some time and recorded the event in her diary. She wrote, "What I saw in the mirror on that day, made me shiver

69

Madame Dubbary, the beloved mistress of the Emperor of France, who had seen her tragic end in the magic mirror of Cagliostro.

with fear. The mirror was showing moving pictures. Emperor Louis XV, the Empress and I featured in those pictures. Cardinal Rohan had told me that Cagliostro is a master fortune-teller. It was for this reason that I invited him to my residence so that I could know my future."

"Count Cagliostro took out a mirror from his pocket. He told me that it was not necessary that what you see in this mirror would be good. If you wish, you can even now change your decision regarding seeing your future. If the mirror shows something that is not to your liking, please do not blame me."

After this the Count recited some *mantras* and invited me to peep into that mirror framed in ivory. I cannot describe what I saw there. I also do not wish to meet Cagliostro anymore.

During the French Revolution, Emperor Louis, his Empress and Madame Dubarry were publicly guillotined by the people of France. Their heads were then jubitantly thrown into the air. This happened in 1774. May be, Madame Dubarry saw this ghastly scene in the mirror on that fateful day.

The real name of Cagliostro was Guiseppe Balsamo. He was born on June 8, 1743 at Pelermo near Sicily. He was born in a poor Jewish family. Being unable to bring up his son, his father abondoned him on the roads to fend for himself, Guiseppe was brought up by a priest in a church. The priest educated him and at the same time taught him to prepare medicines from herbs. Guiseppe was a person given to mischief, and as such he was asked to leave the church. He took refuge with a

*Guiseppe alias
Cagliostro alias
Marchese Pellegrini*

*Lorenza alias
Seraphina
Pellegrini.*

maternal uncle. There he specialised in drawing, but due to his nasty nature, he used this art also in nefarious activities.

Guiseppe fell into bad company and wandered about to learn black magic. He also started making predictions regarding petty matters. In 1768, he got married in Roms to Lorenza, a woman of exquisite beauty.

Guiseppe had to soon flee the country. He got entangled in many court cases. He was charged for duping people, making false predictions and non-payment of loans taken. He had become a notorious figure. As such, he went to Germany with his pretty wife. From there, he went to London. When he reached London, he had already changed his dress and name. In 1776, he had become Marchese Pellegrini and his wife had assumed the name of Seraphina.

Soon, he started telling the winning numbers to speculators. It is not known from where he learnt to predict the numbers, but he could do it quite correctly. His reputation was firmly established in this line. People even forgot his past misdemeanours and flocked to his house to know the numbers and earn easy money. The strange thing was that people did not even hesitate to bribe Seraphina to know the lucky numbers.

He created a lot of enemies during this period, but nobody could get hold of him. He somehow got an old book from Egypt. He started defrauding the people by making prophesies. He used children as medium. His clever strategy was that if the predictions proved to be correct, he was lauded for them. In case, they turned out to be incorrect, he could blame the juvenile mediums.

After some lapse of time, he again changed his name. Now, he called himself Count Cagliostro and immersed in the business of prophesying. His work load increased. It was not safe for him to dupe people. As such, he started to make honest efforts to gain proficiency in his work. As they say, evil habits can hardly be discarded easily. It was difficult for him to resist the temptation of making easy money by duping people.

Cagliostro created waves by predicting the death of an influential person named Scieffort during his sojourn in Nuremberg. Scieffort died within a month of Cagliostro's prophesy and people started taking Cagliostro seriously. During this period of his life, Cagliostro remained busy with black magic and *tantrik* rituals. He achieved some success in this line. He did not make any major prophesy during this period.

Cagliostro went to Poland. There he amazed everyone with a startling prophesy in the court. Incidentally, this prophesy came to be correct when he was living at Warsaw. Emperor Stanislas Augustus was greatly interested in prophesies and occult sciences. He started pampering Cagliostro. A lady member of the royal family did not like the importance being given to Cagliostro. She once said that Cagliostro knows so much about future, he should tell her as to what was in store for her during that month. Cagliostro prophesied, "You shall go on a journey this month. Your carriage will be involved in a minor accident. While waiting for some alternate arrangement, spectators will cause you injury by pelting apples at you. You will go to a pond to clean your clothes and wash yourself. There you will meet a person. In spite of all sorts of initial obstacles, you will be able to get married to him."

This prophesy turned out to be correct. But, Cagliostro was turned out of Poland when he tried to dupe Prince Poninsky with a miracle with the aid of a fake touchstone. He told the Prince that he could convert iron into gold with the help of his touchstone. He tried to replace the iron piece

72

with an identical piece of gold hidden in his palm. He was caught by the associates of the prince while doing so.

It was a tragedy of Cagliostro's life that he took undue interest in misusing his talents. He seemed to have reformed himself after the above misadventure. He started predicting about petty matters like lost or found, life and death, boy or girl, result of examinations and court cases at Strasbourg to earn his living. He got some success in this direction.

In certain matters, he earned fame as well. The widow of an army officer once asked him, "My question is in this closed envelope. Can you give an answer?"

Cagliostro replied, "The boy shall be unsuccessful in his pursuit." The envelope was opened. The question was whether the lady's son would be commissioned in the army.

A young bride asked him about the age of her husband. Cagliostro refused to answer her. Later, it transpired that she had been planted by the administration to test him. He would have been asked to leave Strasbourg if the answer to this question turned out to be incorrect.

A judge asked Cagliostro, "Tell me if my wife is at home or not and what is she doing at the moment ?" After putting this question, he sent his son to his residence to find out what was happening there. Cagliostro told him that his wife is in the house playing cards. Two other women are with her. It turned out to be absolutely correct.

Cagliostro started treating patients in Strasbourg. He built up some reputation in this line as well.

He had predicted the death of the Empress of Hungary and Bohemia in 1780, which proved to be true. "Maria Theresa will live up to the age of 63," he had predicted in a meeting with his critics.

He generally went astray after achieving some success. From 1745, he started invoking spirits and started displaying his occult powers. It is recorded that on one occasion he called thirteen spirits at the same time.

On returning to Paris, Cagliostro again started making predictions. He raised a scare by predicting that Louis XV, his wife and mistress would be guillotined. It came to be true. He also made a prophesy regarding the rise and fall of Napolean, which also turned out to be correct.

Empress Maria Theresa died at the age of 63 as predicted by Cagliostro.

The French General La Marliere was being prosecuted in a court. He was very worried about the judgement. His friends amongst the revolutionaries assured him that he would be given some light sentence and released. He consulted Cagliostro who predicted, "The General would be killed by an executioner wearing the uniform of national Security Forces. He will be sentenced to death." The General was executed and the reputation of Cagliostro soared to new heights.

The desire to indulge in occult practices and control ghosts and spirits took possession of Cagliostro once again. As it is, he used to predict through a medium. This time, he exceeded himself. He was exiled from France on the charge of stealing a diamond necklace of the Empress.

He reached Switzerland with his wife in May, 1787. By this time the police had come to know that Cagliostro was actually Guiseppe who

Emperor Louis XV, his wife and mistress Dubarry were executed by the public as prophesied by Cagliostro.

had changed his name many times. Nearly all the doors were closed on him and nobody paid him any attention.

Cagliostro shifted to Rome with his wife. He again tried to establish himself as a forecaster. His most famous prediction was made regarding the fall of Louis XVI of France. As the sign of his fall became apparent around October, 1789, his reputation reached its peak. As the revolt

Cagliostro became famous as his prediction regarding fall of Louis XVI proved to be correct.

subsided, he was charged with many offences and put into prison. Though the court sentenced him to death, it was changed to life imprisonment on the intervention of Pope. He started counting his days in the prison with his wife. He tried to run away from the prison but was caught in the attempt. He was transferred to the fort of San Leo from St. Angelo prison. He was found dead on August 26, 1795. His wife died a year later.

When the revolutionaries captured the city in 1797, they enquired about Cagliostro. If he was alive, they would have honoured him for he had predicted the success of revolution a long time back. ■ ■

Prophesies from Map

Alexis Mermait, the priest of Saint Prex city in Switzerland, suddenly developed, what can at best be described as sixth sense, in the year 1927.

Mermait was looking at a map. He felt that there was water at the depth of 88' 9" at Pepayan area in Columbia. The water was flowing at an average speed of 500 litres per minute.

Digging was carried out at that place. Mermait's premonition turned out to be correct.

Joanna Southcott: Advent of Messiah

Daughter of an ordinary farmer, she could gather round her a large band of devoted followers. Her followers formed associations and her movement took the shape of a cult. Even now, most of her devotees believe that she would be reborn with added strength. They had implicit faith in her as most of her prophesies turned out to be correct. It is said that she suddenly realised that she had the capacity to unravel the future. Many considered her to be mad, but there were others who believed that she was an enlightened person who had attained siddhi.

A s the executioner put the black cap on the head of the condemned prisoner, she screamed loudly, "You cannot kill me. I can never die. I have Joann's permit to go to heaven."

From the above incident in York in 1809, the authorities came to know that a self-proclaimed prophet Joanna Southcott was distributing permits to the people, entitling them to go to heaven. Actually, at that time Joanna was already a well known fortune-teller. The officers wondered as to why instead of pursuing her flourishing business of forecasting, she had launched upon this dubious work of sending people to heaven. Further investigations were ordered.

When a magistrate with a few constables was sent to contact Joanna in this regard, she came before Philip Scott, the Magistrate, in measured steps and haughty manner. She told him, "Go back to your house. You have left your safe open. If you do not go there immediately, most of your things together with important documents would be stolen. The window of your room has no grills and is open. It is also right on the road."

The Magistrate left her house in hurry. He returned a little later and said, "Joanna, you are a genius. But, I will have to perform my duty."

Joanna remained unperturbed. She replied calmly, "You do your work. I shall continue doing mine. Nothing can stop me from making prophesies and doing social service."

By that time, Joanna had issued 13,000 permits for heaven. She used to say, "I can see that only 1,44,000 people will be allowed to enter heaven on doomsday." People had implicit faith in her as most of her prophesies had turned out to be correct. Hence, there was rush for buying these permits.

Joanna achieved international fame. It was because of a casket left by her. This casket was securely tied with strings and she handed it over to her followers. At that time, she said, "Whenever 24 Bishops of England and Wales meet, this casket may be opened. If this is done the earth shall be free from all crimes, violence, disasters and dacoities." (See Box)

There are still many people in England who have complete faith in what Joanna had predicted. These people have named their associations as 'Southcottian'. They have taken the shape of cult associations.

Joanna was born in April, 1750, in a place called Gittisham in the county of Devonshire. From the very beginning, she was a devout girl who kept herself busy in prayers and worship. Though she had to work for long hours in her father's dairy, she always found time to go to the church and pray. Nothing was remarkable in her life. She led an average everyday existence. One day, while sitting in the church, she suddenly exclaimed, "I am hearing voices. Somebody is talking to me."

It was the day of Christmas. After that Joanna did not behave in any abnormal manner for one year. Then again, during Easter in 1792, Joanna claimed to hear some divine voices in the church. The priests in the church thought that she might have heard voices in a state of high fever. People usually become delirious in high fever. The matter ended there. After a lapse of ten days, Joanna declared that she had the capacity to foretell the future.

The Mystery of the Casket

Nearly two hundred years have passed since the death of Joanna Southcott, but even now her name crops in newspaper headlines. The reason is the mysterious casket left by her which is called 'Joanna Southcott's Box'.

This casket came into the news, when her followers formed the 'Panacea Society' in the beginning of this century. They declared that their messiah has left behind a mysterious and sealed casket as her legacy. She had also directed that if this casket was opened in a meeting of 24 bishops, all the crimes, dacoities and miseries in the world would come to an end. There was also a warning that if the meeting did not take place and the casket remained unopened, the human race is certain to be wiped out.

It is said that a person named Harry Price opened it in 1927. This person was famous for his research on supernatural powers. The casket contained some personal belongings of Joanna like an old cap, a pistol and things of everyday use. Her supporters claim that Price did not open the real casket. It has still to be opened. It will only be opened when the bishops agree to meet. Nobody knows in whose possession this casket is or its present whereabouts. As such, the casket remains shrouded in mystery.

Most of her initial forecasts proved to be correct. Most of them were about mundane matters and were exhibitionist in nature. For example, she used to tell as to where the lost things could be found. She also predicted regarding the crops and their quantity and such petty matters. After some time, Joanna started keeping records of her predictions. They were kept in sealed envelopes. The envelopes were printed with the English letters, I C. There used to be a star over and under these letters in her seal.

Some 46 of her prophesies turned out to be correct in 1793. Her fame travelled far, up to such distant places as Japan and Russia. People started taking her predictions seriously. In 1801, she published her book of prophesies under the title *'The Strange Effects of Faith'*. The book was a roaring success. But, it had one bad effect. Joanna was carried away by her popularity and success. She proclaimed establishment of her own cult or group. Many people came under her influence and became her devotees.

**Joanna used to put this
seal in her predictions on
a sealed envelope.**

In the year 1802, she settled in London. It is here that she started misusing her influence. She became a controversial figure because of her issuing permits for heaven.

It is presumed that by 1805, she had already issued 10,000 such permits. The government became active when her opponents pressurised it to take action against this exploitation of gullible people. The government instituted investigations against Joanna. It so transpired that every enquiry officer became her devotee after meeting her. It was only when Mary Batman, who was sentenced to death on murder charges in 1809, said that she had a permit for heaven given by Joanna, that an uproar started. But, as most of her devotees were her blind followers and had implicit faith in her, she came to no harm.

In 1810, Joanna started constructing special worship centres for her followers who called themselves Southcottians. Some 17 such centres are not only existing at the present time but are active in spreading her cult.

Joanna made a startling prediction at the age of 64. She declared that she would give birth to a new *messiah* in the coming year. The new *messiah*, Shiloh, would show the world a new path. In her third book, *Third Book of Wonders*, she had written at length about this new prophet.

Joanna suddenly fell sick on March 17, 1814. Many well known physicians examined her. They were surprised to find that in spite of her advanced age, Joanna's body was quite young and youthful. She was carrying a four month foetus in her womb. But, the prophet did not take birth. Her condition worsened day by day. She died on December 27, 1814, leaving a large number of followers who were anxiously awaiting the birth of the promised *messiah*.

Joanna had instructed her friend, the famous physician, Dr. Richard Reece, to conduct postmortem on her body, four days after her death. When her body was opened up as per her desire, the famous doctor was surprised to find that there was no baby inside her womb, though she had all the symptoms of a four-month pregnancy. May be, her intense desire to be the mother of a prophet had produced all these symptoms of pregnancy. She might have created these symptoms by auto-suggestion as some people cure themselves by this method. It could also be taken as an example of her supernatural will power.

Her followers buried her in Saint Johns Wood cemetery in Regent's Park. The following words were engraved on her tombstone. "Thou shalt appear in Great Power." In 1874, this tombstone of her grave was shattered to pieces by a powerful explosion. Hopes were kindled in the hearts of her followers that their *messiah* might be re-born. Their hopes were belied as Joanna did not rise from her grave. Her followers have full faith that someday she will again come on this earth. In any case, the reason of that powerful explosion still remains shrouded in mystery.

The Terrified Forecaster

The reputed fortune-teller of Jordan, Sheikh Abdul Rajag, had predicted in 1949 that Abdullah, King of Jordan, would be assassinated in 1951.

His prediction came to be true in 1951. Sheikh Abdul Rajag was so shocked and terrified at his own correct prediction that he has not spoken a word since 1964.

81

Marie Lenormana: The Queen of Soothsayers

She was the queen amongst the soothsayers. She made predictions in an age when forecasting was as serious a crime as treason. But, she never faltered or weakened. She cared little for opposition or the times she lived in. Steadfastly she did her work. She was supposed to be an expert in palmistry, numerology, astronomy and even used playing cards to foretell the future. Arrested for illegally foretelling future, she had to suffer imprisonment for one year. The strange thing is that one who correctly predicted the future of so many luminaries failed to calculate the time of her own death.

The solitary chandelier hanging from the roof provided only a dim light to the underground cellar. One had to strain his eyes to see anything in that semi-darkness. To top it all, dead bats and other animals were hung from the walls of that basement. The atmosphere was eerie. In that peculiar and dreadful atmosphere, a woman was gazing intently at the faces of three men. She looked like a sorcerer. It seemed that she was trying to read or decipher something written on their forehead. Suddenly , she spoke in voice that seemed wierd as well as mysterious. "All the three of you will die in tragic and painful manner."

Then she turned towards one of them and said, "You will be the first to die."

The French history is witness to it that all the three were killed one after the other. It was nearly impossible to imagine at that time that these three people will meet such tragic deaths. The year was 1793. The French

Revolution was at its peak and these three persons were its top leaders. They were the revolutionary leaders Marat, Saint Just and Robespierre and it was unthinkable that they would die soon and that too at the hands of their own people.

As predicted by the mysterious woman in that underground cellar, Marat died first. He was killed in Charlotte Corday. The other two followed him. Robespierre even put that woman in the prison for predicting his death. It is another matter that she was released soon.

This fortune-teller was once walking on the road. Seeing her, a crowd collected and a lot of people stretched their hands towards her to know their future. Stung by curiosity, Josephine, the wife of a general, also stopped there. Seeing her, the soothsayer proclaimed loudly, "Long live the Empress." Old soothsayer had become senile. They started leaving the place. After all had gone away, the woman asked the old fortune-teller, "Do you find something special in me?"

"You shall become Empress of France. Before that your present husband will die. You will remain in prison for eighteen months. Though

Marat was first to be killed as predicted by Lenormana.

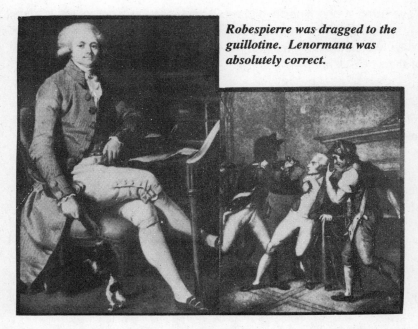

Robespierre was dragged to the guillotine. Lenormana was absolutely correct.

sentenced to death, you shall escape it very narrowly. You shall remarry a warrior. He shall wear a crown resembling a bee-hive. This great man with cropped hair will become the arbiter of the destiny of France," the old soothsayer replied without halting for breath.

Josephine was both happy and sad to hear this forecast. She was pleased that her name would feature in French history. Later, all that was predicted by that old woman turned out to be correct to the last letter.

Who was this old woman? She was Marie Ann Adelaide Lenormana. She was supposed to be the Queen of soothsayers. She was also a palmist and astronomer. She had built up a reputation as being extremely adept in dispelling the darkness regarding the future and bringing it to light.

Lenormana was born on May 27, 1772 in the Alecon province of France. Her father was a favourite courtier of Emperor Louis XV. Her mother was a woman of exquisite beauty. She was looked after by her step-father on the death of her father. With the death of her mother she became an orphan. Her step-father remarried and that severed her connections with that home. She was sent for schooling at the age of seven to Benedictine Convent. Her teachers and school mates soon

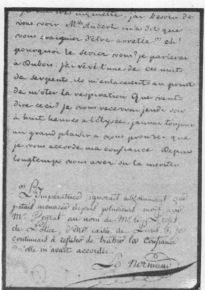

Lenormana (above) and excerpts from her letter to Josephine.

realised that Lenormana had an uncanny capacity to unravel the future. She could tell about the day on which it would rain as also many other things regarding loss of goods, sickness or who was to fall in the slush on a given day. She could also tell as to what questions would be asked in the examinations or who would be punished by the teacher in the class.

Those were the times when it was believed that the power to predict future can only be devil's gift. In order to exorcise her of the influence of devil, she was given a dry bread to eat with water. As luck would have it, there was always someone in the church who wanted to know about his future. These people gave Lenormana almonds, cashewnuts and walnuts. The pockets of her frock were always full of these things. The dry bread also did not go to waste. Who ate them, was apparent from the way the dogs in the church wagged their tails and followed Lenormana.

Lenormana's reputation soared to new heights on account of a prediction she made at the early age of eleven. The post of the 'Mother' at Benedictine Convent fell vacant. Most of the ladies were hopeful of their own appointment or made guesses about it. Lenormana was roaming about that place learning her lessons. She heard the talks amongst the ladies and said that their guesses would prove to be futile, as the Emperor would appoint someone from outside to the post. It turned out to be correct.

Lenormana was sent from one school to another for higher education. She proved to be a talented pupil. After some time, Lenormana opened an astrological bureau with a friend Flemmermont. Here she started making predictions in an underground cellar. We have already mentioned about this room at the beginning of this article.

Though overtly she did the business of selling books, her real business was fortune-telling. People used to come to her shop on the pretext of buying books and then proceeded to the basement, to know their future. Then they left from the back-door. The police and law enforcing agencies were fully aware of this clandestine business, but turned their blind eye towards it. Those days France was smouldering with revolt. The monarchy was in doldrums and the rebels had occupied many places. In such times, any prophesy for or against the ruler or revolutionaries would have invited death penalty on your head. But, undaunted she carried on the work.

In the beginning the washing women took her advice. They would generally ask about the turbulent times and when peace will be restored. They were worried about the stoppage of their work due to revolution. They also brought their domestic problems and wanted to know when they would end. As Lenormana's predictions turned out to be correct they spread the word amongst their friends and acquaintances. Lenormana's business flourished.

Lenormana made many remarkable predictions about many important personalities in France. She predicted that Princess De Lamballe would die a horrible death. She said that a person named Lazara Hosche would be a great general, but he would die early at the age of 30. She had prophesied that Napolean Bonaparte, who was an ordinary officer in the French army, would one day ascend the throne of France as Emperor. His wife would be a beautiful widow of an army officer. From prison, she would directly enter the palace. Three great revolutionary leaders, namely Marat, Saint Just and Robespierre would meet untimely death.

The director of court theatre of the French Emperor, Montansier, had gone to take the advice of Lenormana in her underground office, before he was apprehended by the revolutionary forces. He has recorded, "That woman saw me intently and said that you would be arrested. You

86

As per the prophesy of Lenormana, Napoleon became the arbiter of France's destiny.

Lenormana had prophesied a long time back that Josephine would become the Empress.

will receive many injuries but these injuries would save you from death. When you will be taken to the executioner for beheading, the punishment will be postponed for a few days because of your physical condition and injuries. In the meantime, the revolution would take a new turn and the new Emperor will spare your life."

Montansier was kept in a prison, but he recovered from his injuries before the date set for his execution. In despair, he wrote a letter to Lenormana. She replied, "Bribe the doctor. He would say that you are sick. You will escape execution. Then you will live for a long time and earn fame." Montansier escaped the gallows and for the rest of his life remained indebted to Lenormana.

Napolean Bonaparte had consulted Lenormana in the year 1793. At that time he was quite disgusted with his army job. He wanted to know about his future in France. He also enquired if he would secure the passport for going to Turkey. He was dumbfounded by the replies that Lenormana gave to his queries. Lenormana prophesied, "Why are you in a hurry to leave France? You have been born to become the arbiter of the destiny of France. You have to rule over it. You shall be the Emperor. You will go out of France only to win battles."

87

Napolean did not believe her at that time. Later when the prophesies proved correct he sent her a valuable gift with the message, "Kindly do not see me. I am now busy with my present and have no time for the future. I do not wish to know anything regarding my future."

Lenormana had made one more prophesy on the day Napolean had met her. She had predicted, "A widow shall play an important part in making you happy and influential. Do not betray her and show your ingratitude, otherwise both of you shall be doomed."

Abrantes, a lady member of the royal household has written in her memoirs, "At first, Napolean laughed at his weakness for Josephine in a light manner. Then, he objected to the presence of Lenormana in the palace and said that she should not be called there. Josephine at that time promised that Lenormana would not be called to the palace anymore. But, she continued to meet her secretly and at times consulted her through letters."

The personal secretary of Napolean, De Meneval has written, "He did not like his wife's trust in soothsayers and prophesies. Many times he admonished Josephine on this matter. I was present on many occasions when he bluntly refused to take advice from Lenormana. Once, he felt so angry that he got Lenormana arrested. The Empress always kept it to herself as to what Lenormana told her and she did not even let the cashier know when and how much she paid Lenormana for her advice."

When relations between Josephine and Napolean turned sour and they were on the brink of separation and divorce, the Empress wrote a letter to Lenormana from the palace. In this letter written on November 16, 1809, Josephine wrote, "I am very worried, I have to meet you. Aubert has told me that you expect to be arrested. What are you afraid of? I shall talk to Dubois, the police chief. Last night I saw snakes in my dream. They were entwined round my body trying to crush me. I felt suffocated. What is the meaning of this? ..."

Lenormana sent her a confidential reply, "Within one month it shall happen, though it should not. Try to be brave. This had to happen, it cannot be helped". And, within a month, Josephine and Napolean were divorced.

Another interesting episode. In 1804, a painter came from Sweden to Paris to make some purchase. Out of curiosity, he went to Lenormana to know his future. Lenormana asked him, "If I demand 10,000 francs for

The Coronation of Napolean and Josephine. The seemingly impossible prophesy of Lenormana also proved correct.

the prophesy that I am going to make about you, will you still show me your hand? It is worth that amount."

The painter was bewildered and said, "If I get the above amount in the future, I shall definitely offer it to you. At present, I only want to show my palm to you".

"Then listen, you would be Emperor. You shall rule over two countries and your reign shall last twenty five years," Lenormana predicted in all seriousness.

"How can an ordinary painter become an Emperor," he asked incredulously.

Lenormana started laughing and said, "You are no painter. You are a warrior and an army officer."

This painter was none other than Bernadotte, a Marshal in Napolean's army. In 1818, he became King of Norway and Sweden. He ruled till 1844. Though Bernadotte did not send 10,000 francs to Lenormana in his life time, he left directions in his will that this amount be paid to her.

On December 11, 1809, the police arrested Lenormana. The details of that day are recorded in police records. We give below excerpts from the same.

Only two constables in civilian dress accompanied Inspector Veyret to the dirty underground room, which was full of some, to arrest the old woman. The two were holding Veyret in such a manner that it seemed as if he was dangerously sick and had come to her to know his future.

Seeing them Lenormana said, "I shall not be able to help you. I have to attend to people already waiting for some time. I know, the police is going to arrest me in half an hour's time."

These people were speechless as they heard this. They thought it would be better to tell her the truth. They showed her their police cards. She did not make any protest.

Lenormana was released in a very mysterious manner only a week after her arrest. It is difficult to believe in what Lenormana has written in her autobiography regarding her sudden release. In it she has detailed as to how she terrified the entire police station with the help of a spirit named Areel.

Lenormana was in a very annoyed mood when she made the following prophesy in January, 1810. "The one who rose to be an Emperor from a sepoy will be vanquished in 1814, and will be reduced to the status of a prisoner in an island."

Readers must be aware that Napolean was inflicted a crushing defeat in 1814 and was exiled to the island of Elba, where he spent his days as a prisoner. Lenormana's fame soared to new heights. She brought out a newspaper under the name of *"Souvenirs Prophetiques"* devoted to astrology and prophesies.

In 1830, Napolean's daughter Emilee de Pellapra became a widow. Her mother Leroy advised her to meet Lenormana. Pellapra has written in her reminiscences:-

"According to the advice of my mother, I went to see her dressed in a maid servant's clothes. I tried to look as ugly as possible. The old woman (Lenormana) looked crafty in her black velvet clothes and pock-marked face. She looked at me intently and then continued staring at me for some time. Then she spoke, "You have tried your best to hide your identity, but you cannot hide from me what is written on your face. You are a rich woman. Though you seem to be unmarried, you have recently lost your husband. Your troubles are to end soon. You will remarry and that too before the spring. Do not try to know or search for your would-be husband. At present, I see a large ocean between you. You shall meet him after two months." I laughed at this incredible prophesy of the old woman. I even retold the story to every one in jest."

Pellapra was soon convinced of the powers of that old woman. She was soon engaged to Prince of Chimay. Her fiance travelled to England to meet her.

In the meantime, Lenormana was charged with many offences. Many important people called her a liar, fraud and a gossiper. Things came to such a pass that her work and existence faced extinction.

Bonaparte had recorded this before his death in 1821. "In 1793, she had told me that I shall rule over France till the lure of another marriage does not make me foresake Josephine. This woman had the audacity to write to me in 1814 that if returned to France from the island of Elba, I shall die a respectable death. I have made the prophesy of Lenormana true in all aspects."

Some critics believe that this memoir of Napolean had been faked by Lenormana herself. Many others assert that Lenormana had already achieved a lot of fame as a soothsayer. She had no reason to fake the above. She could hardly derive any benefit from the same.

During her travels to Brussels, she was arrested by the police on April 11, 1821, on charges of indulging in forecasting in an illegal manner. She had to face a prolonged court case that ran for a long time. Eventually, she was sentenced to one year's imprisonment on June 7.

Lenormana was broken-hearted when she came out of the prison. She started writing books and her memoirs. She wrote 34 books on different subjects. It is strange that one who accurately unravelled the future of so many people, could not correctly predict her own age. She had said that she would die at the age of 108 or when she was 123 years. But, she died of heart attack on June 25, 1843, at the age of 71 years.

A critic wrote on the occasion of her death, "She was great, may be, but she was a great soothsayer cannot be easily stomached. After all, she could not even make an accurate prediction regarding her own age or time of death." ■■

James Lees

The detectives of Scotland Yard were able to arrest the notorious criminal Jack, the Ripper, in 1888 with the help of a person who had

divine insight. Jack, the Ripper, had killed many women in different parts of London in a most brutal and horrendous manner. He selected only prostitutes as his victims.

The man who helped the police in locating this gruesome killer was Robert James Lees. It is said that Lees started seeing scenes of the murders committed by Jack, the Ripper, from August. He took the detectives with him to the place where the murderer lived. It is not known, if Lees saw anything with his divine insight after he got that murderer arrested.

Cheiro : The brightest star

If anybody can be described as the brightest star in the firmament of futurology, the pride of place will go to Cheiro. Endowed with an impressive personality with piercing blue eyes. Cheiro proved he had no peer in the five continents, as far as forecasting is concerned. He was the first to claim that the lines on the palm unfold definite tendencies regarding future. He studied thousands of palms and reduced palmistry to an exact science. He made many astounding predictions which brought him eternal fame and respect. He has also written many illuminating books on palmistry and numerology which enable even a layman to understand the meaning of what these lines on our palms indicate.

The entire palace was enveloped in a deathly silence. The then Princess of Wales arrived to enquire regarding the condition of the Prince. "How is he," she anxiously asked.

The entire team of doctors bowed their head but said nothing. The only sound that could be heard was that of the wall-clock and the wheezing sound coming out of the throat of the dangerously sick Prince of Wales, who later ascended the throne of England as Edward VII.

At the same time, a person of impressive demeanour entered the room. He greeted the Princess, and proceeded towards the bed of Edward, without even waiting for her response. He put his mouth near the ear of the Prince and whispered, "I am Cheiro. Do you remember me. He

Nobody believed Cheiro when he said that the dying prince would ascend the throne of England as Edward VII. They had to accept his supremacy as he sipped tea with the King after his coronation.

once met at the Belgrave Square residence of Lady Arthur of the American Society. Do you recollect, your Highness."

The Prince breathed with difficulty and nodded his head in assent.

"Your Highness, you must be remembering that your lucky numbers are 6 and 9. I had also predicted that you will be crowned king in August, 1902. Did I not tell you that you cannot die before the age of 69."

Edward said something in a hoarse voice that sounded like yes. Princess Alexandra confirmed, "Yes, he is saying yes."

Cheiro continued with his efforts, "It is now the month of June. Your coronation shall take place after a month. You have to be all right by then."

The Prince murmured something that could only be understood by the Princess. He was saying, "Whatever you told me in the past came out to be true. I think, whatever you are telling me now shall also prove to be correct."

Cheiro has no peer amongst fortune tellers in all the five continents. His accurate predictions kindled people's faith in fortune-telling, (below) his famous sitting room.

The renowned forecaster Cheiro was happily sipping tea with the King to be, Edward VII on the morning of July 15, 1902, in the royal palace. As predicted, the coronation took place in August.

Cheiro's predictions were based on scientific studies. He was a very self-confident man. There are numerous examples, of the above, that illustrate his genius.

Cheiro went to America in 1893. A sensational case was being heard in American courts at that time. In January, 1894, the court had sentenced the accused Dr. Meyer to die on the electric chair on charges of murder. Those days, Cheiro was studying the changes that occur in a man's life due to changes in the lines of his hand. He got the permission of the prison authorities to study Dr. Meyer's hand. He told him, "You have to live for some time. You shall live in spite of the sentence of execution passed by the High Court. All your appeals will fail, even then you shall live. It shall be a miracle. You shall escape death at the last minute. I do not know whether the charge of poisoning your rich clients

95

The London residence of Cheiro. It is said his spirit resides there.

and embezzling their insurance money is true or not, but I know this much that your life will be spared." He further continued, "You are only 44 years of age, doctor. You have still to live for another fifteen years. You will die in a hospital bed of some ailment."

Prior to his day of execution, the Supreme Court found some legal lacuna in his death sentence. His execution was stayed by a special order. The American papers gave full prominence to this story. Cheiro became a hero in the eyes of all the people.

A month before this incident, Cheiro earned fame in another matter. He had just reached America and set up business in the fashionable locality of Fifth Avenue. Fisher, correspondent of the popular newspaper *New York World*, placed before him palm impressions of seven people. He challenged Cheiro to give details regarding these unnamed persons. He assured him that if he predicted correctly, his paper will give him full credit and praise him to the skies.

On November 25, 1893, after studying the impressions, Cheiro confidently said, "The first hand is of a political leader, who will prove to be an astute administrator. He should be occupying an important post. The second is that of a clever lawyer who is also occupying a high post. The third hand is that of a writer who should be a woman. The fourth and fifth hands are of artists, who will earn fame in singing. The sixth hand is also of an artist, probably a musician. The seventh hand is of a criminal, who will be sentenced to death. He will escape capital punishment and later die of sickness."

A full page of the Sunday issue of this paper dated November 26, was devoted to the praise of this palmist. The main page carried headlines

Mark Twain, the famous writer. His effort to hide his identity from Cheiro's penetrating eyes failed.

that Cheiro can tell correct things regarding total strangers by only seeing their palm impressions. The interesting thing is that the seventh hand belonged to Dr. Meyer who had been sentenced to death and whose story has already been related earlier.

There are innumerable stories regarding Cheiro's genius in fore-telling the future. Once, he was travelling in a train. He started reading the palms of his fellow passengers to pass time. His eyes widened as he saw hands of his fellow passengers. Most of the passengers' life line ended abruptly. Cheiro did some thinking and got down from the train at the next station. The train met with an accident, resulting in many casualties. Hardly anyone doubted his prophesies. Mrs. Leiter, a billion-aire of Chicago, went to Cheiro with the impression of a hand. She told him that it was the impression of her daughter's hand and asked him to tell her future.

Cheiro said, "This girl will marry someone who is a ruler in an eastern country. But she will die an early death."

Mary, the girl in question, was soon married to Lord Curzon, Viceroy of India. Later she died at an early age.

The well known writer, Mark Twain, once went to see Cheiro *in cognito*. Cheiro was able to tell him in no time that he was a world fame personality who was hiding his identity. He further said, "You shall earn fame as a writer. Your name should start with letters 'S." This was absolutely correct. The real name of Mark Twain was Samuel L. Clemens.

Mark Twain was greatly impressed by Cheiro's capacity. In the words of Mark Twain, "Whatever he told me was perfectly true. I started as a journalist. Then, I did not complete my favourite writings. I had travelled a lot."

"My wife edited my writings. She became invalid after falling in snow. It was correct. My secretary would try to entrap me. My wife Livy would die in 1904. Everything was true."

Mark Twain wrote the following comments in Cheiro's visitors' book, "Cheiro expostulated my character in such a manner that I felt ashamed. I thought that I would say nothing about his penetrating genius, but in the end I had to accept it."

Cheiro was born on November 1, 1866, in a place called Bray in Wicklow County of England. His birth name was John Warner. Later, he changed his name to Louis Le Warner Hammon. He adopted Cheiro as his name when he decided to make future-telling as his profession. His father was supposed to belong to the royal family of Normandy. His mother was French. His mother had great interest in astrology and because of this Cheiro also got interested in this science.

From the very beginning, Cheiro was very good in forecasting future. Once, he was reading some book on astrology in his school library. His teacher also came there. He asked Cheiro to read his future in order to test him. He had to admit that Cheiro possessed ample talents in this line.

Cheiro was always engrossed in astrology from an early age of twelve. Once, he was travelling to Liverpool. One person, who saw him reading a book on palmistry, asked him to read his palm and tell his future. Cheiro said, "There is one unique similarity between your's and Napolean's hand. And that is that your fate line ends abruptly."

"What is the meaning of this peculiarity?" asked the man.

"It is clear. One more Napolean will be exiled to St. Helena."

"And what would be the reason for my misfortune?" the man asked again.

"Certainly a woman," replied Cheiro, "I can see that your line of heart is crossing your fate line, at the same spot from which your line of fate disappears."

The man caressed Cheiro's head and said, "This is not possible my child. I am so busy in my work that I have no time for women."

He gave his card to Cheiro as he alighted from the train. It read Charles Stewart Parnell. He was a top leader of the Irish people. After some time, Cheiro, who was now an adolescent, learnt that Parnell was being entangled in a court case regarding his relations with a pretty widow named Catherine O'shia and his political career was on the brink of disaster. This incident boosted the morale of Cheiro. He started collecting palm impressions of thousands of people. Amongst them were the famous and the notorious, successful men and failures, criminals, murderers, advocates, officers, teachers, dancers, bearers, hotel and shop owners and judges. This proved very helpful in his future work.

His father sent him to London when he was seventeen. But, he came away to India. In Bombay, he met Ved Narain Joshi, an astrologer. Joshi took Cheiro to meet many *tantriks* and astrologers of Himalayas, Varanasi, Ladakh and Kashmir. After three years of travel in this country, Cheiro returned to England. He had by now gathered a huge treasure house of knowledge in this line.

Cheiro set up his office in Bond Street in London. The very first day, Arthur James Balfour, president of London Psychical Society, who was passing by, stopped at his office, out of curiosity. He asked Cheiro to forecast his future.

Whatever Cheiro told him was absolutely correct. He said that one day you shall be the most important political leader of the country.

Balfour became prime minister in 1902. He remained in this post till 1905. Most of the friends of the prime minister made a big line to Cheiro's house. But, Cheiro never took any undue advantage of his proximity to the seat of power.

Cheiro attained unparalleled popularity and reputation within a short time. His attractive personality, blue magnetic eyes, deep manly voice, immaculate clothes and a well appointed office contributed a lot to his success. He became extremely busy and fell sick due to overwork.

In his *Reminiscences,* he has written, "I made a cardinal rule in my profession. I used to tell about the past life of the person who came to know about the future. The reason being, that the person would be convinced that one who could tell about the past so correctly, would also read the future correctly."

He lived in America for one year before returning to his native land. About his experiences in America, he has recorded the following, "The Americans asked me only two questions. They were, when would I become rich or when would I make a marriage of my choice." Both men and women invariably asked these two questions.

On his return to England, Cheiro won more plaudits. The newly appointed Chief Justice of England, Russel of Killowen, called him on the day of his assumption of office. He told Cheiro, "Three years back you had prophesied that I shall get my coveted job on July 19, 1894. I am amazed as to how you could calculate things so exactly." The news of Chief Justice's appreciation of Cheiro's competence was another feather in his cap.

The Tsar of Russia had shown his hand to Cheiro in 1904. At that time, Cheiro had predicted that the year 1917 would be the most unfortunate for him. Tsar had gone *in cognito* to see Cheiro. During the end of that year, he invited Cheiro to his palace in St. Petersburg. The Tsar asked, "Do you still think that the year 1917 would be the most fatal year for me."

Rasputin (above) died in the manner predicted by Cheiro. Cheiro's premonition regarding the Tsar's tragic end turned out to be correct.

"I am sorry that I had to say such a thing," Cheiro replied. Readers must be aware that the Bolshevik Revolution under Lenin took place in 1917 and the Tsar and most of his family members were killed.

During his travels in Russia, Cheiro also met the powerful *tantrik* Rasputin, who had sinister influence over the Tsarina. He told Cheiro in a commanding tone, "I have no desire to know about my future, but I wish to test your capacity to forecast. Tell me, my future."

Cheiro replied without hesitating for a moment, "I can see that your end will come due to palace intrigues. You will be first poisoned, then a man shall stab you. Another person will shoot you. I can see your corpse floating on icy water."

Rasputin was greatly enraged at this prophesy. He left the place saying that if Cheiro had not been a guest in his country, he would have arranged to have his body thrown into icy water.

Cheiro had foreseen his end correctly. Rasputin, who had become the most powerful man in Russia and who had complete control over Tsar Nicholas and his wife, died exactly in the manner that Cheiro predicted for him.

Earlier, Cheiro had correctly predicted the death of Herbert Kitchener, a high ranking naval officer in England, in a naval accident in the month of June at the age of 66. He had also foretold Humbert I, King of Italy, in 1900 that he would be assassinated by a terrorist within three months.

In August, 1900, Cheiro had told the Emperor of Persia in Paris, "Riots have broken out in Teheran. People have arrested the governor of Teheran. These riots have erupted due to unprecedented rise in the price of wheat and bread."

Once, the fearless adventurer Sir Ernest Shackleton, went to see Cheiro, promising to be a musician. He wanted to test his capabilities. Cheiro studied his hand and declared, "I think you are a born leader. You think nothing of playing with fire. You are a dauntless adventurer well-known throughout the world. The tragic thing is that you shall die at the age of only forty eight years in a hazardous expedition." Sir Shackleton died on January 5, 1922. During his expedition to Antartica. Cheiro had really peeped into his tragic end.

The courageous adventurer Sir Ernest Shackleton was correctly told by Cheiro that he would die in an adventure at the age of 48.

Many important and influential persons have testified about the Cheiro's uncanny insight into future. Many, who went to him as sceptics, came back as believers in his capabilities. One such person was Sir Edward Marshall Hall. Cheiro had predicted about his victory in the elections, eighteen months before the event. He had confidently told him that he would win by 209 votes and that proved to be the margin of his victory. It seemed as if he could visualise this event eighteen months in advance.

Cheiro wrote a number of articles after visiting the war fronts during Sino-Japan war (1894-95) and Russian-Japanese war of 1904-05. He travelled many times to China, Russia and India. He collected some 19,000 rare books and was the author of many books and articles on palmistry and numerology.

Life was not bed of roses for him. He was declared insolvent in 1910 due to betrayal and conspiracy of some people. He had to pass through bad times for one year. He was now a tired man and his mental state was that of an exhausted person.

Cheiro married Mena Dixon Hartland when he was 54. He had very cordial relations with the famous spy Matahari. He had told her that 1917 was an unlucky year. She fearlessly faced the execution squad in

Versailles. It is supposed that she knew of her death because of her friendship with Cheiro, and as such was fully prepared to meet it.

Cheiro had predicted, much in advance, regarding the Soviet-China treaty of 1925; agitations and strikes in England during May, 1926; civil war in China, earthquake in Channel Island in July, 1926; and fire in many large buildings in England. He had prophesied that the political and military capacity of Italy would enlarge during 1927-29 and Africa would be its target and the period of 1928-30 would not be lucky for Emperor George V of England. He had already told that the Emperor would remain bed ridden for a long period. In 1927, he had forecast that Duke of York, the second son of King of England will be the future Emperor and he will ascend the throne in 1936. He had already made a prediction regarding the Prince of Wales, that he would ascend the throne as Edward VIII, but would abdicate due to his love for a woman.

Cheiro had written, "The 20th century will witness the rise of socialist thought in many countries. There would be a lot of changes in the governments during this century. The common people will come to power. The church will not remain untouched by this revolution. The Jews will demand their independent nation and Israel will come into existence. There shall be a long drawn out war in that region."

He had predicted in 1931, "By the end of this decade, a world war will break out. India will be free, but there shall be bloody strifes between

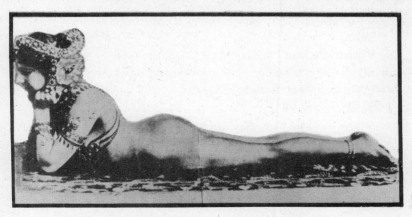

Matahari, the German spy, a friend of Cheiro knew about her time of death.

Like Nostradamus, Cheiro had confidently predicted about the abdication of Edward VIII.

the Hindus and Muslims in which many would die. The war between France on one side and Italy and Germany on the other is certain in this period. America will be entangled in a war with Japan. The result shall be horrendous. Ireland will undergo a civil war." We need not emphasise that all these forecasts turned out to be correct to the last letter.

Cheiro died on October 8, 1936, after a prolonged illness. His residential house still stands as his monument. It is said that his spirit still wanders about in that house. ■■

Did Indira Gandhi have Premonition Regarding her Death?

Mrs. Indira Gandhi was on a visit to Bhubaneswar on October 30, 1984. She had to address a public meeting at that place. During her speech, she suddenly said something that was quite out of context. In a trembling voice she said, "If I lose my life for the country, every drop of my blood shall strengthen the nation."

Only twelve hours after this speech, her bullet-ridden body lay at 1, Safdarjung Road. She was on her way to give an interview to a foreign TV network. The ground was red with her blood. By the time she was rushed to All India Institute of Medical Sciences, she was dead. Her own security guards had killed her. Amongst the documents found in her papers was a half-written will. It seemed that she had started writing her will only a few days before.

Did she have a premonition regarding her death. Did she know she might die soon? The above quoted lines from her speech point towards it. There was no occasion or provocation for her for that emotional outburst.

Amrita Pritam, the famous writer and poetess has written:-

"Indiraji called me to her residence at about 6.45 p.m. on September 30. I spent an hour with her. We talked about security arrangements for her. She seemed a little restless and said, 'Yes, I think there are some weak spots here'."

Amrita Pritam continues, "The night of October 27. I was sleeping, I dreamt that the orb of light changed into a ball of smouldering fire. Then I heard a few explosions. It was the same sound, the same cosmic sound, the same visual when Indiraji was shot at ... I find myself on the staircase of a fort. They were hundreds of foot steps going down. She stood somewhere in the middle. She seemed to have emerged from some room on the right ... Suddenly she vanishes and the stairs are vacant, enveloped in darkness."

Amritaji is a serious type of writer and meticulously keeps her daily diary. She has mentioned many such dreams and mysterious experiences in her writings.

In her memoirs, Amrita Pritam has clearly mentioned as to what Indira Gandhi thought regarding her security arrangements. From her reply given to Amrita Pritam on the subject, a doubt is created in one's mind. Did she have some prior knowledge regarding her death?

Kraftt: A Political Astrologer

He did a lot of research before he ventured into the profession of astrology. He found that a man's fortune is affected by the fate of his other family members. Not only that, he analysed the data of deaths and births and reached certain conclusions. He studied cosmic influence on human nature. Though he was forced to make false prophesies in favour of Hitler and Nazi Germany, he amply proved that he could also make astounding genuine forecasts. He used Nostradamus' predictions to the advantage of Germany by twisting and misinterpreting them, and was able to demoralise Allied Powers during Second World War. He was the favourite astrologer of Hitler but he proved that he was not a mere puppet in his hands.

The year 1942. A middle aged man was present in the secret room of Adolph Hitler on January 8. Hitler was pacing the room. He had his hands knotted at the back and seemed worried. One could easily discern that he was in an agitated mood from the frown on his forehead. Suddenly he stopped and asked, "You have predicted my future many times. But, you never told me that a trusted friend will desert me. If you know, tell me clearly till what time Germany has to face reverses in war."

The man hesitated for some time and then replied, "Till May, 1945."

"And what about my future?"

Eva Braunn who committed suicide with Hitler.

Hitler married Eva Braunn on April 29, 1945, only a day before his death. Krafft knew that Hitler would have to commit suicide.

"Shining like sun's rays and secure as a bunker,"

A slight smile could be discerned on Hitler's face. He picked up a large piece of chocolate from his table and put it in his mouth. Then he asked," When will be the enemies of Germany demoralised and finished"?

"I have already told you Fuhrer, by May, 1945," was the ready answer.

Hitler burst into a loud laugh and again asked, "I hope this prophesy is not like other fake prophesies that you make for our propaganda under Goebbel's directions."

"It is genuine, you shall realise that later."

Karl Ernest Kraftt had really forecast correctly that day. It was another matter that he had made them in a garbled manner on account of Hitler's wrath.

The half-burnt bodies of Hitler and Eva in the bunker.

Hitler married his beloved Eva Braunn on April 29, 1945, in a bunker in Berlin. Both of them committed suicide the very next day. Hitler never realised that he was Germany's worst enemy. He had already instructed his subordinates to pour petrol on their dead bodies and put them to fire after their tragic end.

It was only on April 13, that Goebbels had told Hitler that the American President Roosevelt had died. Hitler felt elated and commented, "He was correct. He told me that the enemies of Germany will be finished by April." Kraftt had been dead for nearly three months.

Nobody knows as to when and how Krafft met Hitler. The world came to know of his close relations with Hitler in the year 1939. Five

Goebbels, head of Propaganda department took full advantage of Krafft's predictions.

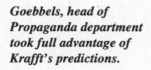

108

Krafft's book based on fake prophesies of Nostradamus.

College days picture of Krafft.

more astrologers were working for Hitler at that time. The prominent amongst them were Wolf, Ellich, Ludwig and Frau Elsbeth Ebertin. Ebertin is the same lady who had predicted about Hitler's rise to power in 1924 itself.

Kraftt came to know Virgil Tilea, a minister in Rumania in the year 1937. Tilea was greatly impressed by Kraftt's extraordinary capabilities in predicting future events. He even corresponded with him regularly. It was through Tilea that he came in contact with influential people.

Kraftt was born in Switzerland on May 10, 1900. He started having premonitions regarding coming events from his childhood. He predicted about the death of his only sister. He was supposed to be a talented student who had special flair in Arithmetic. He joined the army at the age of 20. There, he started a club in which he and his friends practiced reading thoughts of each other. It was then found that Kraftt had extraordinary divine powers in reading other's mind.

He got admitted in Geneva University in November, 1920, for higher studies. During his stay in Geneva, he came to the conclusion that the destiny of a person is influenced by the fate of other members of the family. He collected statistics from the Birth and Death office and analysed them. When he put up his analysis and conclusions before important people, they made fun of him.

He studied Cosmic influence and its effect on human nature. He also prepared horoscopes of some 4,000 people according to their professions. He ventured into the work of forecasting after making all these studies and enriching his knowledge. Kraftt named his technique of making predictions 'Cosmobiology'. He could not get his degree and in January, 1926, had to accept a job in his friend's publishing house to keep his body and soul together. He also prepared horoscopes for people to earn extra money.

In 1928, Kraftt wrote two books which were published in France and Germany. Kraftt was considered to be one of the many well-known forecasters after the publication of these books. During 1923, he became a close friend of Dr. Heinrich Fesel, who worked as an officer in the seventh section of the State Security Headquarters named Reichssicherheitshauptant. Fesel was incharge of using prophesies to the advantage of Germany. Dr. Fesel started paying a fixed amount to Kraftt under Hitler's directions. In return, he had to make some prophesies every month, keeping in mind the interests of Germany.

Kraftt had even laid down the auspicious time for Germany's attack on Poland and Western countries. Kraftt even determined the age and manner of death of German officers and soldiers by studying their horoscopes. Those who seemed to have longer life, in his view, were selected for hazardous and dangerous tasks.

In a letter written on November 2, 1923 to Dr. Fesel, Kraftt said, "The life of Fuhrer is in danger between the 7th and 10th of this month. I think a bomb blast will take place when he would be in a public meeting. His life can be saved if proper precautions are taken."

Dr. Fesel could not gather courage to tell higher authorities regarding this prophesy. Dr. Goebbels had also issued instructions that any prophesy regarding danger to the life of Fuhrer should not be given any prominence.

Hitler was taking part in some annual celebrations in Munich on the evening of November 8. He somehow got the news of this prophesy. He left the place earlier. There was a loud explosion on the dias as soon as Hitler left the place. Eight persons were killed. 20 persons, including some armed guards who were near the dias were injured.

110

Rudolph Hess, the right hand man of Hitler. If Hess had paid no attention to Krafft's prediction, the death of Hitler was certain.

It was the commonsense of Hitler's trusted associate, Eudolf Hess, that saved him that day. Kraftt had written directly to Hess mentioning his prophesy and asking him to save the Fuhrer.

The German leaders started courting Kraftt after this prediction. Kraftt's reputation spread throughout the world. From January, 1940, Kraftt was generally seen with top German leaders and took part in many diplomatic and political functions. On such occasions, Kraftt was introduced in the following manner, "Meet Karl Ernest Kraftt. He is man responsible for saving Fuhrer's life. He had foretold what was going to happen that day. It was because of his capabilities that the Fuhrer was saved at the eleventh hour."

It was at this time that Kraftt's capabilities and the confidence that he had earned amongst the people began to be misused by the authorities. An edition of Nostradamus predictions published in 1968, was brought out in Germany. His prophesies were twisted in such a manner that they favoured Germany. Attempt was made to demoralise the people of enemy countries by these cooked-up prophesies. Handbills containing these prophesies were air-dropped into enemy countries.

In this fake edition, Nostradamus was made to prophesy: "In the war, the artillery of German army would be totally ineffective on the population and area of South-East France." As this prophesy was air-dropped, there was a rush amongst the people to go to South-East France. When the German troops entered France from North-West, the way was clear for them.

It started a sort of astrological war between the two sides. Ian Fleming, the famous English novelist hit upon such a plan that nullified Germany's astrological assault. Fleming arranged to smuggle such magazines into Germany that predicted the downfall of Hitler after April, 1941. It was shown that his stars were on decline. On the other hand, Rudolf Hess was made to believe that he was going to be the initiator of peace talks between England and Germany. The thought that he (Hess) was going to attain status of a world figure because of these efforts was continuously instilled in his mind. Hess became victim of these tactics and flew to Scotland to initiate peace talks. Hitler was enraged when he heard of this and prohibited publication of prophesies, making it illegal.

In spite of Hitler's anger against fortune-tellers, Krafft remained close to him. Krafft's antecedents were checked and it was found that he was not a spy. On June 13, 1942. Krafft was asked to prepare horoscopes and predict the future of English, American and Russian leaders, Generals and Admirals.

By this time Rudolf Assietz had become the favourite astrologer of Hitler. Assietz had black penetrating eyes. He brushed his hair backwards and was always sowing doubts about others in Hitler's mind. Hitler also deputed another astrologer named Herr F. G. Goerner to keep an eye on Krafft.

Once, the renowned Commander Field Marshal Rommel met Krafft and asked, "What have you to predict about me."

"You are a great general and a very brave person. But, you will not die in a battlefield. You will select to die in a manner that is not meant for a warrior like you", Krafft replied.

When Rommel told Hitler regarding this prophesy he simply laughed. After some time, in 1944, Hitler forced Rommel to drink poison as he suspected that Rommel was conspiring against him. At that time Rommel must have realised that Krafft did not only make false prophesies for Germany.

Krafft had predicted an unnatural death for Field Marshal Rommel. He had to take poison on orders from Hitler.

Kraftt had been imprisoned. On January 8, 1945, Kraftt prophesied, "His days are numbered. I am dying of cold and sickness without any treatment. I am not being set free. But, he will also die. The end of April, 1945, is also his end. I am counting my last breaths in Lehterstrasse prison. He will commit suicide in a bunker."

For the last time, Kraftt had made another true prediction on the day of his death. ■ ■

Jeane Dixon: Fifty-fifty Forecaster

Jeane Dixon is counted amongst the top forecasters in the modern age. Some of her predictions have been amazingly correct. At the same time, many of her prophesies have proved to be damp squibs. That is why we have called her a fifty-fifty forecaster, as the percentage of her incorrect predictions is also quite high. Many people have charged her with being an agent of the Central Intelligence Agency of America. In any case, people still look upon her a reliable forecaster. It points to the fact that there must be something special in this woman.

Jeane Dixon's name was heard for the first time in connection with a prophesy she made regarding Franklin Delano Roosevelt, the then President of United States of America. President Roosevelt came across her in 1944 and casually asked her during the talks, "How long have I to live?"

Blue-eyed and extremely pretty, Jeane Dixon replied in a solemn manner, "Six months or even less."

When President Roosevelt died suddenly on April 12, 1945, the White House authorities got published in the papers the details of her meeting with the late President in 1944. Instantly she came into prominence. In this meeting, Dixon had also prophesied, "Chine will be a communist state and prove to be the biggest thorn in America's side. The African continent will also be an area of worry on international level."

Jeane Dixon, the world famous American fortune-teller.

Jeane Dixon (*nee*Pinkert) was born in 1918 at a city named Wisconsin. She had to shift to California with her family at an early age. She was hardly nine when people discovered that Jeane possessed the capacity to foretell future. She advised Marie Dressler, an actress, not to severe her connections with the stage. Dressler was disappointed with her career and thought of starting a hostel and giving up acting. Accepting Jeane's advice she continued acting on stage. Later she became a highly sought after star. She also got opportunities to act in films produced in Hollywood. Readers must be aware that Hollywood is the epicentre of American film industry.

She was active in business during her youth. She did business in real estate. But, she also made many prophesies in spite of her preoccupations with her business. During a reception in 1945, she told the Indian military attache Sher Ali that "India would be divided into two countries on February 20, 1947. Today it seems to be unthinkable, but it will prove to be correct."

In the same year, she told Churchill, the most popular and successful war time Prime Minister of England, that he would not be Prime Minister after the war. Churchill laughed at her and said, "The people of England have tested my capacities and it can never happen." Churchill's conservative party was defeated in the elections held after the war and the Labour leader Clement Atlee became the Prime Minister.

She had already predicted a year before it actually happened that Mahatma Gandhi would be assassinated by a Hindu fundamentalist in the year 1948. Those who knew about this prediction had to bite their nails, when Gandhiji was killed by Nathuram Godse. She also earned fame when she published details regarding the rise of Anwar Saadat in Egypt and his assassination under a well laid conspiracy.

In 1956, Jawaharlal Nehru, the then Prime Minister of India asked Mrs. Dixon, "who shall be the Prime Minister of my country after my death." She replied, "A short-statured man whose surname shall start with the letter 'S' ''. When Lal Bahadur Shastri became Prime Minister after Nehru, Mrs. Dixon's fame spread far and wide. She was now looked upon as a trusted forecaster.

Mrs. Dixon had predicted in 1956 that in the coming year Soviet Union will launch a satellite into the space. It will successfully orbit round the earth and then will be retrieved. She had also predicted that Khrushchev will assume power in Soviet Union at a time when he was just an ordinary leader in the Soviet Communist Party. During September, 1961, she made another astounding prediction. She said that a prominent actress of Hollywood who was supposed to be a sex symbol

Franklin Roosevelt

Winston Churchill

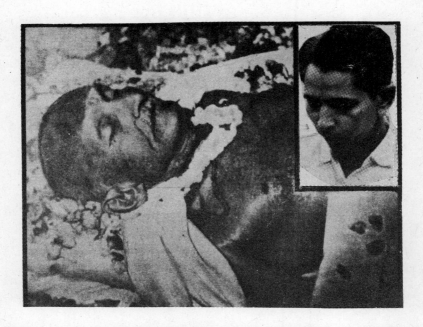

Jeane Dixon's prophesy that Mahatma Gandhi would be assassinated by a fanatic proved to be true. (inset) Nathuram Godse.

would commit suicide. Her name and surname both start with letter 'M'. A correspondent asked, "When will this happen?" "Exactly within one year," was her confident reply. This occurred as predicted by her. Hollywood's sex symbol, Marilyn Monroe, killed herself by taking an overdose of sleeping pills.

In an interview given to the famous international magazine *Parade* in 1956, Mrs. Dixon said, "A tall, blue-eyed youth with thick brown hair shall occupy the White House as President in 1960. He would be the youngest President to take oath, but he would be killed during his tenure as President."

Jack Anderson, a journalist, who was interviewing her then asked, "How have you come to this conclusion?" Mrs. Dixon gave the following reply, "I saw this vision while praying in St. Mathew Cathedral. It was raining at that time."

Mrs. Dixon tried many times to warn John F. Kennedy after he was elected President, of the coming danger, but she failed to convey it to him.

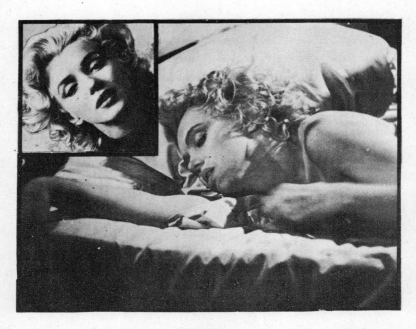

As per prophesy of Jeane Dixon, Marilyn Monroe, the sex symbol of Hollywood, committed suicide within one year.

In 1957, she phoned to Shah Feisal of Saudi Arabia that a conspiracy was being hatched to kill him. But, before he could think about this warning and take action, Feisal was killed.

Mrs. Dixon peeped into a mysterious Crystal Ball to know about the future. Many of her prophesies have proved to be false.

In 1980, she had predicted that in the year of the appearance of Halley comet, America will have a woman as President. She also said that Mrs. Margaret Thatcher will not last as Prime Minister for a long time. She is now thinking of third term. She predicted that between 1988 and 1990, the crown of England will pass to Prince Andrew from Prince Charles. The Shah of Iran will flee Iran due to revolution but will stage a come-back. She made many incorrect prophesies regarding the future of India in a book published in 1981. Her reputation suffered a lot due to these prophesies.

Regarding her predictions that have proved incorrect, she has to say this, "I do not know why some of my prophesies have proved to be

True and false prophesies regarding important personages
1. Khruschchev will come to power (right); *2. Lal Bahadur Shastri will be the Prime Minister* (right); *3. Prince Andrew would be nominated Prince of Wales* (wrong); *4. The Shah of Iran will stage a come back* (wrong); *5. Margaret Thatcher will not remain Prime Minister for a long time* (wrong); *6. Shah Feisal would be assassinated* (right); *7. The rise and fall of Anwar Saadat* (right).

*The prophesy made by Jeane Dixon regarding Kennedy, made in the
presence of newspaper columnist Jack Anderson, proved to be correct.*

wrong. I get up at three in the morning and at that time try to see the future.
Whatever, I sense at that time, I tell the people. I have never claimed that
all my predictions would be correct."

She had predicted in 1978 that a great war will break out around
1980 and a period of peace shall begin in 1999. She also said that Russia
will enter Iran and Palestine. China would start germ-warfare against
America. She also predicted that a leader belonging to rural area will win
power in India and will show a new path to the country as Gandhi had
done in the past.

Her critics assert that Jeane Dixon might have been gifted with
divine insight only on some occasions. It seems now it has deserted her.
No reason can be given for this. ■ ■

120

Joan Quigley: Advisor to a President

The whole world was amazed to know that Ronald Reagan, President of America, did everything according to the advice of astrologers. The timing of all his administrative and political decisions were set by astrologers. It can be said that he did not move a step without their concurrence. The newspapers started intensive investigations. The F.B.I also investigated the security aspect of the matter. They wanted to know if state secrets were being divulged under the smoke-screen of astrology. The results must have been sufficient to flummox their officers.

"**T**he President should remain extra alert, cautious and under foolproof security on March 31, 1981," — these were the last lines of a letter received by Nancy Reagan, wife of American President Ronald Reagan. The letter had come from California. Mrs. Reagan saw the name and address of the sender and kept it in a safe place. The matter was soon forgotten. But, something happened two months after this prediction that made President Reagan and his wife believe in astrology.

52 days after the receipt of this letter, President Reagan was coming out of the Hilton Hotel from a door reserved for very important personalities, after addressing the representatives of the American Labour Federation. A twenty five year old youth started shooting towards him with a .22 bore pistol. A bullet hit Reagan's left lung. The second bullet pierced the head of his Press Secretary James Bready. Two other bullets hit a security officer and a police constable.

Reagan was fortunate to escape death by the skin of his teeth. He had to undergo two minor operations. A few hours after, he was seen smiling on the TV screen. He waved to the viewers and was signing papers.

Nancy Reagan again read that letter received in March, during the night. It said, "After analysing the time when the President assumed office, I came to the conclusion that the third month of his tenure should be dangerous. He may have to face a murderous attempt in a public place. The conjunction of planets on March 31, is very strange. The President should be very alert, cautious and under extremely strict security on March 31, 1981."

President Reagan was lying on the bed. Tears welled up in the eyes of Nancy Reagan. She started looking into the papers written by Carrol Righter. There was not even a slight indication of such an incident between March 20 to March 31. According to Carrol it was a good period for Reagan. He had just won the election for presidentship. If his period was bad, how could he be elected as President of America during this

Unsuccessful assassination attempt on President Reagan by John Hinkley. John Quigley had predicted it earlier.

122

period. Nancy had consulted her astrological advisor Carrol Righter immediately after the receipt of the letter regarding danger to Reagan's life. She wanted to know if there was even a slight chance of the letter-writer's premonition proving true. Carrol denied it vehemently. She said, "Impossible. This can never happen."

In April 1981, Nancy went to the house of that letter writer in a friend's aeroplane. Carrol Righter was not seen in the White House after that. Nancy now started making frequent phone calls to San Francisco which is 3000 miles away from Washington. Mrs. Joan Quigley was now her new advisor in matters regarding future. She talked to Joan at least thrice a week on phone. She took her advice on all matters for seven uninterrupted years.

Joan Quigley was a manly woman of 65 years. Her face was full of wrinkles and she wore over-sized and baggy clothes. When she went to White House for the first time, the security people had to use X'ray equipment to check her. Nobody knows how much money was paid to this woman, with bobbed hair, from the secret account of the President.

President Reagan arranged his inaugural ceremony at the time suggested by his astrologer.

123

Reagan and Nancy: Puppets in the hands of Joan Quigley.

In spite of the best efforts of CIA the Reagan couple never stopped taking advice of Joan Quigley. Nancy became a little more cautious. She stopped using the phone and established direct personal contacts with her.

Quigley did not consult any almanac or any such thing to divulge future events. She used to feed the relevant data to a computer. The computer did all the calculations. The detectives were more worried on this count.

No authoritative information is available regarding the early life of Joan Quigley. Only one thing is certain that she entered this profession of prophesying as a hobby. She was a devotee of Nostradamus.

Quigley advised Reagan on all matters. Her advice was sought on all matters under the sun. She foretold him about the chances of the success of a particular mission. Reagan even sought her advice on economic matters. She directed him regarding places that he could visit and at what time. He was even instructed regarding which foot should be put out first, while getting out of the car. The limit was that she advised Reagan to keep some lucky charms with him. Reagan always carried four or five in his pocket.

Reagan was an extremely superstitious person till he became Governor of California. He has accepted this fact in his autobiography.

Joan Quigley, without whose advice nothing is done by Reagan family.

When his previous astrologer, Carrol Righter, died in 1988, he recorded, "The first thing that Nancy and I consulted each morning was what she had recorded or told about that day."

On one occasion, somebody asked Reagan about the time of his birth on February 6, 1911. His cryptic answer was, "Nobody, except my astrologer has the right to know that. If that is discussed my opponents will have my horoscope cast and start taking advantage of the unlucky periods to launch their attacks on me."

He had chosen the time of his inauguration as Governor with the advice of his astrologer. The time fixed was 11.10 in the night. Most of the people were bewildered when they got the invitation for this function. Reagan was firmly convinced that he was successful on account of the good advice he received from his competent astrologers.

The world would have never known regarding Reagan's faith in

125

Political Leaders and Astrologers

The number of people engaged in the profession of astrology is as follows: There are 5000 in America, 800 in Soviet Union, 3,000 in Japan and approximately 20,000 each in India and China. In Australia, people even consult astrologers regarding their pet animals. The entire expenditure of a small nation can be met from the amount that is involved and spent in this business of forecasting. According to a survey, nine out of ten newspapers carry column of forecasting in nearly all the countries irrespective of the fact whether the country is industrially advanced or under-developed. It is not only the common people or business class that have trust in forecasting. Contractors, doctors, political leaders, advocates, priests and even criminals have faith in destiny. That is why this business flourishes at all times. In the world of films, top as well as struggling artists are always taking astrological guidance. Even those who do not have faith in astrology know their date of birth and zodiacal sign. This can be taken as a symbol of their faith in this science. In matters of marriage, whether it is settled by parents or through computers, it is generally ascertained that the couple's horoscopes tally.

It was for the first time that predictions regarding natural calamities were made on the basis of astrology, after taking into account the conjunction of planets, in Babylonia in 600 B.C. This area is now called Iraq. In 2nd century Ptolemy divided planets into groups on astrological basis. It was then calculated as to how these zodiacal groups were reacting with one another at a particular time on a person. This indicated his destiny. Ptolemy had made a correct prediction regarding death of Harold, King of England, in a war. But, Ptolemy committed a blunder. He believed that the moon and stars orbit round the earth.

prophesies. It was disclosed to the world at large when the chief of White House, Donald Reagan, contacted Nancy Reagan to fix up the President's programmes. Nancy told him, "You can fix any date or time, but let us know two or three days in advance so that we can find out if the appointed date or hour is auspicious or not."

According to Donald Reagan, "Their programmes kept on changing. Many times the security people thought that their programmes or journeys have been cancelled due to frequent changes in timing. Many times, the security people had to do three to four rehearsals on different routes. Even, then, we were never sure."

When this matter was discussed, Quigley said, "I am a serious professional. My work is absolutely scientific. Whenever Mrs. Reagan asked me about the safe time for anything, I told her. Astrology is a complicated affair. The common men cannot understand it. I calculate things after studying the movements of the sun and the moon and then present my conclusions."

Who went to Quigley for advice? Were there politicians amongst them? In this regard, she said, "It is my privilege not to divulge the names of people who come to me for advice. I have never disclosed the names of my clients. What I tell them, remains a secret. Making predictions is no offence. The desire to know the future is not a crime."

In another interview she has said, "My relations with the Reagan couple are due to peculiar reasons. People are always making fun or criticising it. I do not like it. I can assure you that no psychological analysis can reveal more about a person, than I can after reading his horoscope."

On the other hand, Donald Reagan has observed, "An occasion arose when I started keeping diaries with coloured and secret symbols. I kept record of auspicious times for the President for speeches, conferences, talks, travels and public meetings in this diary."

Ronald Reagan had implicit faith in astrological calculations. This is apparent from the fact that he insisted that he would meet Mikhail Gorbachev, President of Soviet Union at only 1.30 in the afternoon in 1987.

When Donald Reagan disclosed the fact of President Reagan's faith in prophesies in May, 1988, it created a storm in diplomatic circles. The White House tried to contradict the news. But, at the same time, Nancy said something during her talks with a newspaper correspondent that nullified these attempts. She said, "What is strange if we have faith in prophesies. After all, everything is done in the interest of the President."

On May 5, 1988, FBI officers raided her San Francisco apartment on instructions from higher authorities. Quigley was not in the house. She

President Reagan chose the exact time, suggested by his astrologer Joan Quigley to meet President Mikhail Gorbachov of Soviet Union.

had left for France. As per her calculations, an earthquake was to hit San Francisco at that time and devastate it. She was happy when it did not happen. Little did she realise that an earthquake had really hit it — a political earthquake. Though San Francisco escaped devastation, Reagan's political future was in shambles. This was known when the election results came in. ■ ■

PALMISTRY, ASTROLOGY, NUMEROLOGY & VAASTU

 **PRACTICAL PALMISTRY**
80/-
size, pp: 365
available in Hindi

 **Palmistry for Beginners**
Discover the mysteries of Palmistry
88/-
Demy size, pp: 282

 **Palmistry of Romance**
80/-
Demy size, pp: 180

 **Marriage-Matching Astrologically**
60/-
Demy size, pp: 142

 **Astrology for Layman**
80/-
Demy size, pp: 184

 **Explore the Astrology** *New*
96/-
Demy size, pp: 200

 **LAL KITAB** Rare Book On Astrology
195/-
size, pp: 336
(bound)

 **INSTANT HAND WRITING ANALYSIS**
75/-
Demy size, pp: 152

 **THE PROPHECIES OF NOSTRADAMUS**
60/-
Demy size, pp: 160

 **Healing Power of GEMS AND STONES**
80/-
Demy size, pp: 136

 **Fascinating world of DREAMS** And what they mean to you
60/-
Demy size, pp: 144

 **PRACTICAL HYPNOTISM**
75/-
Demy size, pp: 236
Also available in Hindi

 **ADVANCED HYPNOTISM**
120/-
size, pp: 264

 **Hypnotism for Beginners** Easy techniques to practise hypnotism
68/-
Demy size, pp: 160

 **Self HYPNOSIS For a better Life**
88/-
Demy size, pp: 184

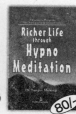 **Richer Life through Hypno Meditation**
80/-
Demy size, pp: 107

 **NUMEROLOGY** A Complete Guide to Understanding and Using Your Numbers of Destiny KEY TO YOUR INNER SELF
88/-
Demy size, pp: 272

 **Numerology of Romance**
80/-
Demy size, pp: 222

 **Horoscope Reading**
135/-
size, pp: 248

 **PREDICTIONS FOR A NEW MILLENNIUM** 1996 to 2012
88/-
Demy size, pp: 272

 **Benefits of Vaastu & Feng Shui**
80/-
Demy size, pp: 144

 **CHAKRA & KUNDALINI WORKBOOK**
96/-
Demy size, pp: 264

 **Vaastu Corrections without Demolition**
60/-
Demy size, pp: 92

 **Numerology** know your lucky numbers for every sphere of life
68/-
Demy size, pp: 120

 **BODY Language**
80/-
Demy size, pp: 120
(Also available in Hindi)

POSTAGE: RS. 15 TO 25/- EACH

3

SELF-IMPROVEMENT

68/- Demy size, pp: 160
Also available in Hindi and Bangla

60/- Demy size, pp: 136
Also available in Hindi

48/- Demy size, pp: 64
Also available in Hindi

48/- Demy size, pp: 80
Also available in Hindi

Demy size, pp: 156

Demy size, pp:

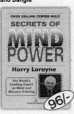

96/- Demy size, pp: 184

96/- Demy size, pp: 192

96/- Demy size, pp: 240

60/- Demy size, pp: 240

120/- Demy size, pp: 304

Demy size, pp:

60/- Demy size, pp: 128

80/- Demy size, pp: 218

80/- Demy size, pp: 174

68/- Demy size, pp: 176

80/- Demy size, pp: 140

Demy size, pp.

80/- Demy size, pp: 155

120/- Demy size, pp: 128

68/- Demy size, pp: 176

68/- Demy size, pp: 176

80/- Demy size, pp: 136

Demy size, pp

POSTAGE: RS. 15 TO 25/- EACH

Big size, pp: 168

12

SELF-IMPROVEMENT

Abhishek Thakore's

31 Mantras for Personality Development

...a tip a day to better yourself

60/-

...y size, pp: 104

The Portrait of a **Complete Man**

80/-

Demy size, pp: 176

The 4-Lane Expressway to **STRESS MANAGEMENT**

68/-

Demy size, pp: 112

The Book of **Etiquette and Manners**

A comprehensive guide to good manners and courtesies

68/-

Demy size, pp: 136

The Secrets of **Marital Bliss**

80/-

Demy size, pp: 176

How to **integrate the self**

Harmonise your body, mind and soul

80/-

Demy size, pp: 112

...ught-Provoking **JOKES**

80/-

...y size, pp: 176

The Portrait of a **Perfect WOMAN**

80/-

Demy size, pp: 128

WITH 8 BESTSELLERS TO HER CREDIT

SECRETS OF HAPPINESS

Tanushree Podder

India's Leading Author on Mind, Body and Soul

80/-

Demy size, pp: 192

Hello! Just married OR about to marry?

All your questions answered in Love, Sex, & Marriage

80/-

Demy size, pp: 144

365 GEMS FOR HOLISTIC LIVING

A DAILY DOSE OF INSPIRATION

ALAN COHEN

195/-

Demy size, pp: 376
(Hardbound)

The Art of **Happy Living**

96/-

Demy size, pp: 168

...eedom from ...hought

96/-

...y size, pp: 160

TALES OF WISDOM

Morale-building, 57 Tales for Children

60/-

Demy size, pp: 160

50 Moral Tales ...from The Gurukul

Fifty thought-provoking stories narrated by a Guru to promote moral values amongst children

60/-

Big size, pp: 160
(In 2 colour)

The Portrait of a **Super Student**

How best to perform in Studies, Sports & Co-curricular activities

80/-

Demy size, pp: 160
(In 2 colour)

7 Mantras to Excel in EXAMS

Prabhu Raj & Sudha Shukla

Prolific writer, Educationist and Management Consultant

80/-

Demy size, pp: 160

Boost Your Brain-Power

Dr G Francis Xavier, PhD
The Great Motivator

96/-

Demy size, pp: 144

...Immortal **Sayings**

96/-

...y size, pp: 192

2000 TITBITS & SATIRES

TO MAKE YOU GRIN, SMIRK & LAUGH

68/-

Demy size, pp: 176

Notable Quotes and **Noble Thoughts**

60/-

Demy size, pp: 96

A Treasury of **Inspirational Thoughts**

68/-

Demy size, pp: 144

The Book of **Uncommon Quips & Quotations**

80/-

Demy size, pp: 128

The Book of **COMMON & UNCOMMON PROVERBS**

Over 1,000 fully annotated proverbs

96/-

Big size, pp: 128

The Complete Guide to **MEMORY MASTERY**

HARRY LORAYNE

Big size, pp: 312

POSTAGE: RS. 15 TO 25/- EACH

CAREER/STUDENT DEVELOPMENT/MANAGEMENT

Demy size, pp: 136

Demy size, pp: 256

Demy size, pp: 120

Demy size, pp: 128

Demy size, pp: 138

Big size, pp

Demy size, pp: 200

Demy size, pp: 120

Demy size, pp: 120

Demy size, pp: 288

Demy size, pp: 208

Big size, pp

Demy size, pp: 144

Demy size, pp: 200

Demy size, pp: 184

Demy size, pp: 248

Demy size, pp: 138

Big size, pp

Big size, pp: 188

Demy size, pp: 176

Demy size, pp: 392

Demy size, pp: 128

Demy size, pp: 128

Big size, pp

POSTAGE: RS. 15 TO 25/- EACH

Demy size, pp: 192

6

Bite-sized bits on **common-sense management**

Gerard Assey

150/-

Big size, pp: 100

Mastering **Salary** Negotiations

96/-

Demy size, pp: 96

WINNING **Résumé**

80/-

Demy size, pp: 136

GROUP **DISCUSSION** For Admissions & Jobs

88/-

Demy size, pp: 200

Business Ideas you can turn into Cash

80/-

Demy size, pp: 128

Multiple **Career Choices** For Graduate & Post-Graduate Courses

135/-

Big size, pp: 280

Secrets of Leadership

Insights from the Panchatantra

80/-

Demy size, pp: 136

Sure **Success in Interviews**

80/-

Demy size, pp: 152

QUIZ BOOKS

MATHEMATICS QUIZ BOOK

60/-

Demy size, pp: 216

Environment **Quiz Book**

48/-

Demy size, pp: 176

ASTRONOMY QUIZ BOOK

48/-

Demy size, pp: 208

BIRDS & ANIMALS QUIZ BOOK

60/-

Big size, pp: 128

MEDICAL QUIZ BOOK

48/-

Demy size, pp: 192

Electronics & Computer Quiz Book

48/-

Demy size, pp: 260

HISTORY Quiz Book

60/-

Demy size, pp: 232

QUIZ TIME

80/-

Big size, pp: 208

Pre-School Primers

first step of:
Alphabet
क • ख • ग
Numbers
Nursery Rhymes
Birds & Animals
Vegetables
& Fruits

Price:
Rs. 15/- each

All books fully coloured and illustrated. Can be cleaned & wiped off.

PICTURE BOOK OF **ALPHABETS**

36/-

SCIENCE QUIZ BOOK

60/-

Demy size, pp: 192

Over 4000 Quizzes 143 Topics
GLOBAL Quiz Book

96/-

Demy size, pp: 256

General Science, Physics, Chemistry and Biology
4000 Quizzes All Illustrated

80/-

Big size, pp: 240

Discover India Series
TAMIL NADU Quiz Book

40/-

Demy size, pp: 160

HEALTH, NUTRITION, YOGA, BEAUTY & BODY CARE

Demy size, pp: 176
Also available in Hindi

Demy size, pp: 112
Also available in Hindi

Demy size, pp: 112
Also available in Hindi

Demy size, pp: 128
Also available in Hindi

Demy size, pp: 120

Big size, pp: 112

Demy size, pp: 200
Also available in Hindi

Demy size, pp: 128

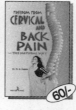

Demy size, pp: 128

Demy size, pp: 100

Demy size, pp: 224

Big size, pp: 128
Also available in Hi

Demy size, pp: 192

Demy size, pp: 120

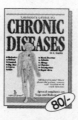

Demy size, pp: 176

Demy size, pp: 126

Demy size, pp: 124

Big size, pp: 144

Demy size, pp: 160

Demy size, pp: 144

Demy size, pp: 112

Demy size, pp: 152

Demy size, pp: 96

Big size, pp: 144
Also available in Hi

POSTAGE: RS. 15 TO 25/- EACH

8

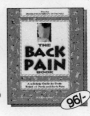

my size, pp: 120   Demy size, pp: 192   Demy size, pp: 128   Demy size, pp: 144   Big size, pp: 428   Big size, pp: 228

my size, pp: 152   Vol-I: pp: 140 • Rs. 96/- Vol-II: pp: 224 • Rs. 135/-   Demy size, pp: 128   Demy size, pp: 224   Big size, pp: 232   Big size, pp: 152

my size, pp: 96   Demy size, pp: 240   Demy size, pp: 136   Demy size, pp: 116   Big size, pp: 224   Big size, pp: 224

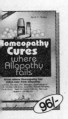

my size, pp: 224   Demy size, pp: 224   Demy size, pp: 120   Demy size, pp: 136   Big size, pp: 208   Big size, pp: 184

POSTAGE: RS. 15 TO 25/- EACH

HEALTH, BEAUTY CARE, HERBS & POPULAR SCIENCE

Youthful Forever
80/-
Demy size, pp: 248

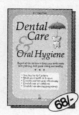
Dental Care & Oral Hygiene
68/-
Demy size, pp: 136

Slim & Smart Body
60/-
Demy size, pp: 128

Home-made Herbal Cosmetics
68/-
Demy size, pp: 128

Your Diet After 50
68/-
Demy size, pp: 152

Fit & Fine in Body & Mind
Big size, pp: 232

You are What you Eat
80/-
Demy size, pp: 184

Better Sex the Herbal Way
68/-
Demy size, pp: 128

Diet in Diseases
69/-
Demy size, pp: 104

Laughter the secret of good health
60/-
Demy size, pp: 120

Safe-n-Sure Weight Loss Programme
96/-
Demy size, pp: 132

The Magic of Massage
Big size, pp: 176

Ayurveda for All
120/-
Big size, pp: 224

Over 1000 Health Hints for One & All
80/-
Big size, pp: 168

Health & Wellness
120/-
Big size, pp: 304

Yoga for Health & Personality
120/-
Big size, pp: 124

Fruitful Meditation
80/-
Demy size, pp: 96

Fact Book in Herbs
Discover the Amazing power of:
- Brahmi
- Ashwagandha
- Spirulina
- Vilayati Imli
- Salai guggal
- Amla

Demy
Price: Rs. 30/-
Postage: 10/- each

Popular Science & Science Tricks

71 New Science Projects Self-learning Kit
120/-
Big size • pp: 120
Also available in Hindi (With CD)

Electronics Projects for Beginners
96/-
Big size • pp: 196

101 Science Games
48/-
Big size • pp: 120

101 Science Experiments
48/-
Big size • pp: 120

Bathroom Science Tricks
36/-
Big size • pp: 104

Kitchen Science Tricks
Big size • pp: 104

10

POSTAGE: RS. 15 TO 25/- EACH

SPIRITUAL HEALING, REIKI & ALTERNATIVE THERAPIES

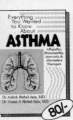

Demy size, pp: 168 — 80/-

Demy size, pp: 280 — 88/-

Demy size, pp: 240 — 88/-

Demy size, pp: 180 — 68/-

Demy size, pp: 242 — 96/-

Demy size, pp: 264 — 96/-

Demy size, pp: 64 — 36/-

Demy size, pp: 144 — 80/-

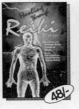

Demy size, pp: 104 — 48/-

Demy size, pp: 304 — 108/-

Demy size, pp: 264 — 108/-

Big size, pp: 264 — 135/-

Demy size, pp: 84 — 48/-

Demy size, pp: 112 — 68/-

Demy size, pp: 200 — 80/-

Demy size, pp: 112 — 68/-

Demy size, pp: 128 — 68/-

Big size, pp: 168 — 96/-

Demy size, pp: 144 — 80/-

Demy size, pp: 136 — 60/-

Demy size, pp: 128 — 60/-

Demy size, pp: 200 — 96/-

Demy size, pp: 272 — 195/-

Demy size, pp: 112 — 68/-

POSTAGE: RS. 15 TO 25/- EACH

11

DICTIONARIES & ENCYCLOPEDIAS

Big size, pp: 48
(In colour)
40/-

Demy size, pp: 136
60/-

Big size, pp: 231
120/-

Big size, pp: 58
(In colour)
72/-

Demy size, pp: 196
48/-

Big size, pp: 520
380/-

Big size, pp: 384
360/-

Demy size, pp: 344
120/-

Demy size, pp: 128
60/-

Big size • pp: 52 (In 4 colour)
Deluxe Binding
Also available in Hindi
100/-

Demy size, pp: 352
68/-

Demy size, pp: 184
50/-

Demy size, pp: 456
88/-

Demy size, pp: 128
60/-

Demy size, pp: 152
24/-

Demy size, pp: 104
60/-

Demy size, pp: 128
48/-

Demy size, pp: 232
68/-

POSTAGE:
RS. 15 TO 20/- EACH

Bloomsbury Dictionaries

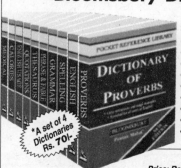

- Dictionary of Phrase & Fable
- English Thesaurus
- Spelling Dictionary
- Dictionary of English Usage
- Medical Dictionary
- Dictionary of Calories
- English Dictionary*
- Dictionary of Grammar*
- Dictionary of Proverbs*
- Dictionary of Quotations*

*A set of 4 Dictionaries Rs. 70/-

Pocket size • Pages: 256
Price: Rs. 30/- each • Postage: Rs. 10/- each

12

COMPUTER BOOKS

Big size, pp: 224
Also available in Hindi

125/-

Big size, pp: 520
(FREE CD-ROM, SMS Joke
Book & Mouse Pad),
Also available in Hindi

175/-

Big size, pp: 448

175/-

Big size, pp: 520

195/-

Big size, pp: 224

60/-

Big size, pp: 144

95/-

Big size, pp: 136

99/-

Big size, pp: 264

68/-

Big size, pp: 360/-

195/-

Big size, pp: 192

68/-

Big size, pp: 416

195/-

Big size, pp: 444

225/-

Big size, pp: 392

225/-

Big size, pp: 184

90/-

Big size, pp: 252

125/-

Demy size, pp: 296

Robert McG 140/-

Demy size, pp: 164

120/-

RAPIDEX Straight to the point series

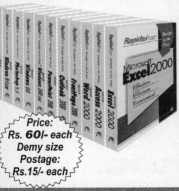

**Price:
Rs. 60/- each
Demy size
Postage:
Rs.15/- each**

Microsoft Excel 2000
Access 2000
Word 2000
FrontPage 2000
Outlook 2000
PowerPoint 2000
Windows 2000 User
Windows 98
PhotoShop 5.5
WindowsNT4 User
Flash 4

RAPIDEX Condensed Users Guides

**Price:
Rs. 140/- each
Big size
Pages: 216 to
316 each**

Core Java 2
Windows NT Server 4
Java Script & VB Script
Windows NT 4 Workstation

13

FUN, FACTS, HUMOUR, MAGIC & HOBBIES

Demy size, pp: 184

Demy size, pp: 115
also available in Hindi

Demy size, pp: 152
also available in Hindi

Demy size, pp: 112
also available in Hindi

Demy size, pp: 104
also available in Hindi,
Bangla, Kannada &
Assamese

Demy size, pp: 11
also available in Hindi

Demy size, pp: 104

Demy size, pp: 176

Demy size, pp: 128

Demy size, pp: 152

Demy size, pp: 128

Demy size, pp: 12

Demy size, pp: 124

Demy size, pp: 115

Pages: 144

Pages: 120

Pages: 200

Demy size, pp: 248
(Hardbound)

Big size, pp: 112
(Full colour book)

Demy size, pp: 112
also available in Hindi,
Kannada and
Marathi

Demy size, pp: 124
also available in Hindi

Demy size, pp: 124
also available in Hindi,

Demy size, pp: 124
also available in Hindi

Big size, pp: 120
also available in Hindi

POSTAGE: RS. 15 TO 25/- EACH

14